1916: The Blog

A Book of Humor
By Christian Schneider

Pelham Press, LLC
P.O. Box 5372
Madison, Wisconsin, 53705

Everything in this book actually happened.

Except the stuff that didn't.

Praise for 1916: The Blog

"A lot of books predict the future; **1916: The Blog** actually predicts the past. A smart, observant satire with unexpected heart, it's the funniest book you'll read all year, depending on what year you read it."

-**Davy Rothbart**, author, MY HEART IS AN IDIOT, creator, FOUND *Magazine*, and contributor to *This American Life*

"Christian Schneider's **1916: The Blog** is a wildly inventive concept that mixes historical research, a keen eye for social satire, witty writing, and giggle-inducing humor that is reminiscent of the history jokes from Rocky and Bullwinkle, classic Bloom County comic strips, and maybe a touch of "Bill & Ted's Excellent Adventure." Offbeat, madcap, unpredictable and a whole lot of fun."

-**Jim Geraghty**, *National Review*

"A clever, funny frolic of a book that reinvents the 'historical comedy' genre, Christian Schneider's **1916: The Blog** conceives of an internet far more entertaining than our own."

– **Karol Markowicz**, *New York Post*

To Mara, Cole, and Finn.

Prologue

Time present and time past

Are both perhaps present in time future,

And time future contained in time past.

I've been thinking a lot about this T.S. Eliot passage in the two weeks since my grandfather passed. He was nearing 90 years old, so nobody could accuse him of not living a full life. He was a salty old crow, fiercely independent – which allowed him to live in his own home until the very end. When he went, he left an attic stuffed with old boxes and artifacts from his life. Yet neither my father nor any of my aunts and uncles seemed particularly interested in methodically combing through papers and documents from more than a half-century ago. So, I took on the task.

The climb into the musty attic was difficult. Given my grandfather's advanced age, I guessed that there's no way he had touched anything up there in at least three decades. I dove into the first box I could find. It contained the type of ephemera one would expect from a lifetime of careful record keeping. There was a receipt from when he had his car's oil changed in 1954. In 1974, he wrote the McDonald's corporation to complain about the company recasting the character of Grimace as a good guy. They sent him a coupon for a free cheeseburger that, almost certainly out of spite, went unused.

As I moved through the boxes, I saw one that appeared to have some of his paraphernalia from World War II. As I pulled the box toward me, I saw an old chest underneath. Considering that people put their most valuable items in such sturdy chests to protect them, I immediately cleared it off and set out to open it.

On top of the chest, still faintly visible, the name "Sebastian" was painted in yellow. When I lifted the top, there were some old, yellowed papers bunched against the sides of the chest next to what appeared to be an antique typewriter of some kind.

But this old typewriter was different than those I had seen on television shows about antiques. On top of the keyboard were places for several light bulbs; one was still affixed in a socket, one was broken in half. Two cords ran from the back of the typewriter; one was clearly a power cord, while another frayed cord almost appeared to be for a telephone. A third cord ran from the right side, attached to a wooden block that housed a small wooden ball. Underneath the device, the words "York Connectivity Co., Kearney, Nebraska" appeared, along with the year "1915."

Puzzled, I began skimming some of the papers contained within the chest. They were arranged by date, beginning in the year 1916. Many of them were signed "Sebastian." Not only was that not my grandfather's name, he wasn't even born until 1927. Why would my grandfather be in possession of something belonging to "Sebastian," and what was this weird machine, anyway?

The first mystery was solved easily. Sebastian Schneider was my grandfather's father, born in Milwaukee in 1889. Clearly, my grandfather kept this device as a favor to his old man.

My own father didn't have much recollection of Great-Grandpa Sebastian. He recalled maybe he worked as a reporter for a newspaper or something, but sadly, he died in 1948, the same year my father was born. Through the years, our family has spun the yarn that Sebastian's death was due to loneliness brought on by the death of his wife just three weeks prior. But my foray through old coroner's records disputes this romantic tale. To be generous, let's just say Sebastian died of a broken heart. And falling out of a third story window may have contributed.

But my Internet searches couldn't find any mention of the "York Connectivity Company" from Kearney, Nebraska. I took photos of the weird typewriter-like device and showed them to one of the staff members at the State Historical Society, with no luck. He said he had never seen such a thing. I e-mailed the photos to typewriter experts across the country, with no satisfactory response. Everyone was stumped.

Then, one day, I received an anonymous e-mail with the tip I had been seeking. This nameless individual told me to search the recesses of the Historical Society for a 1937 book called Clandestine Government Flimflammery by little-known conspiracy theorist Tierney Buxton. So, I did.

According to Buxton, in late 1915, the York Connectivity Company discovered that not only could telephone cords carry voice information, they could also carry data encoded by sound sent over those same wires. The company began a quiet trial of their new product, hoping to test it to see how users would take to the new technology. They produced roughly 120 of the machines, requiring each user to sign a confidentiality agreement; if the machines didn't work, York didn't want word getting out before they could fix the bugs.

Information being a finite resource, newspapers moved quickly to crush this service. The possibilities were endless; if consumers were allowed to share news stories with one another at no cost, it would jeopardize newsprint's near-monopoly status.

Thus, the large media corporations, led by magnates like William Randolph Hearst, spent untold sums on lobbyists, buying congressmen willing to outlaw the sharing of text over phone lines. In late 1919, Congress passed a law not only outlawing data sharing but also mentioning it in public or in print, so citizens could never even be aware such technology existed.

The media conglomerates, who at the time knew President Woodrow Wilson had suffered a severe stroke and was incapacitated, threatened to divulge this information to the public if the bill wasn't signed into law. Fearing America would be outraged if they learned the first lady was actually secretly serving as president, Edith Wilson quickly signed the bill in private.

And thus, according to Buxton, the first "Internet" was dead. (Buxton was later arrested for trying to smuggle four lobsters in his pants into a movie.) Congress would later accidentally revoke this law when a resolution honoring the 1991 World Series champion Minnesota Twins mistakenly deleted 2,652 pages of the federal code.

Yet for a brief period of time, this communication network was up and functioning. And it appears I may now be in possession of the only evidence to prove it.

And now, with this book, you are also in possession of the evidence. What follows are the unedited network postings of my great-grandfather, Sebastian Schneider, during the year 1916. As Edward Thomas once said, "The past is the only dead thing that smells sweet." Hopefully, although he died more than sixty years ago, these writings grant him new life.

January 1, 1916

Is this thing on?

I have recently come into the possession of the queerest of machines! It is a small wooden box that, when opened, reveals a typewriter flanked by an array of light bulbs and vacuum tubes. And yet, despite its simplicity, I have been told it will revolutionize the way humans interact with one another.

Imagine the panoply of possibilities! Evidently, this futuristic contraption allows one to sit in his home and type messages that are then transferred to other people within a network comprising those with similar machines. Who can conceive of what will happen when useful information is shared during the course of these conversations! Rumor has it that at least two people within this current "web" of users even have access to sets of encyclopedias. A complete world of knowledge – or "INTER-LOGS" – now available at our fingertips!

Imagine, reader, all the erudite conversations and sharing of facts that are soon to follow now that we are interconnected.

I have been told that the existence of this machine is still very much a secret. In order to obtain one, a customer must sign a lengthy document deemed the "terms of service" that prohibits speaking publicly about the machine. It also states the manufacturer is not liable if someone says something untoward or salacious using the machine – but imagine the public condemnation if someone were to utter a baseless, licentious comment about another human being! Who would run such a risk?

From what I have ascertained through discussions, only around one hundred individuals or so have been granted the machines, as they are currently being operated on a trial basis. Perhaps we have unknowingly subjected ourselves to a grand experiment in interlocution. In order to own one of these remote conversation devices, one must also have a home equipped with a telephone line. Evidently, the same small electronic signals that carry human voices over great distances can also be used to transmit instructions to a machine to type words on a remote person's behalf – it is as if your home is equipped with its own telegraph machine! Consequently, the devices have come to be known as "FINGER-PHONES."

You may ask, "How did a man of limited means like yourself come by one of these rare FINGER-PHONES?" As it happens, the device was gifted to me by my fellow worker, Otto Kleiner. Otto, recognizing the vast potential of a device that allows one to communicate with dozens of other like-minded individuals at once, entered the lottery and was chosen to receive a FINGER-PHONE.

My dear Otto thought the educational possibilities were endless for his sixteen-year-old son, so he placed the machine in the young man's room. But one night, Otto walked in the room unannounced, only to be met by his son diving into his bed and hastily wrapping himself in his blankets. On the FINGER-

PHONE, a transmission was coming through from a publication called "Shaved Portu-GALS." Imagine that! An education on the cultural follicular styling of the native Portuguese. Here in America!

For some reason, Otto was displeased by his son's quest for knowledge about the faraway European lands and labeled the contraption a "demon box." His opinion was recently buttressed by the news that some high school-aged children were sending messages to one another expressing a strong desire to ice skate with one another while holding hands. They were all immediately expelled.

Aside from these complications, Otto also complained about how difficult and expensive the machine was to have fixed. When it ceased operating in June of last year, Otto sent a letter to the manufacturer, the York Connectivity Company in Kearney, Nebraska. They replied, telling him that a representative would be there sometime between Tuesday and November, as the mechanic had to ride a donkey to his house.

When the representative finally arrived, he asked Otto whether the FINGER-PHONE was plugged in. Otto answered in the affirmative. The mechanic then turned it off, and then on again, at which point the FINGER-PHONE started up and operated smoothly. For this six minutes of work, Otto was then charged a $454 trip fee plus an extra $276 "donkey fee."

Rather than retain a machine that was corroding both his pocketbook and, for some reason, the morals of his family, Otto bequeathed it to me. And if you are reading this right now, you, too, have begun to tap the untold potential of the FINGER-PHONE.

Had my dear Otto gifted me the device only a year ago, it would have done no good, as I only recently obtained the means to operate a telephone in my home. Soon, the telephone will turn forty years old; it was in 1876 that Alexander Graham Bell issued the first spoken message to Thomas Edison over a short wire in Boston. Since that time, more than eighteen million miles of telephone wire have been laid and, according to one company, nearly twenty-five million messages were transmitted just last year!

You may ask, then, what is the benefit of the FINGER-PHONE over a normal voice conversation? Isn't hearing a person's voice crucial to a meaningful colloquy between chaps? How meaningful it is to hear either the pleasure or pain in someone's voice whether they are 1,000 feet away or 1,000 miles away! It is reminiscent of the most wondrous fiction of H.G. Wells.

Yet the appeal of the FINGER-PHONE is in both its permanence and its wide distribution. When a message – this one, for instance – is sent to other users, each individual's machine types it out on paper, where one may ruminate upon its true meaning. Then, another user may take the time to craft a thoughtful response, to be disseminated by telephone line and automatically typed out for all the other members of the network, or for only one individual within the community. The initiating conversationalist may then respond to the response, usually by comparing their challenger to a bloodthirsty, murderous world leader such as Genghis Khan.

So while telephone conversations are more personal, they are fleeting. However, the permanence of FINGER-PHONE discussions can also be detrimental. According to one report, a neighbor saw a man being chased around his backyard by his gardening hoe-wielding wife as he attempted to light a handful of FINGER-PHONE-printed papers on fire. Evidently, his thirst for global knowledge led him to investigate the late-night libidinous activities of a widow in Springfield, Illinois.

This new invention, however, is simply the latest technological breakthrough in information dissemination. Books, newspapers, and magazines give us views of the world, but they are produced by a small group of the learned. The recorded voice still only fills the homes of the wealthy, as a Victrola costs as much as my monthly salary.

Perhaps one day, the FINGER-PHONE will take the place of more traditional methods of laypeople forcing their voices into the public square. Until this machine, regular folks wanting free speech were relegated to modern technologies such as nailing a flyer to a pole downtown. Others have taken advantage of more recent advances, such as screaming things at passersby on the street. (While effective, this method isn't particularly efficient, as it takes a great deal of time to yell the same point at different people all day.)

One particularly promising feature of the FINGER-PHONE is that it allows people within the network to retain their anonymity when discussing important issues. What a benefit! It is known that the great Benjamin Franklin often used different aliases while writing for newspapers because it allowed him to showcase his brilliance in public, yet remain a layperson among the streets of Philadelphia. Imagine the unrestrained stream of intelligence that will emanate from my tele-machine when other conversationalists are unencumbered by identity!

That is not to say that anonymity does not have its drawbacks.

Recently, it was rumored that one thirty-two-year-old FINGER-
PHONE using gentleman struck up quite a friendship with a
fourteen-year-old boy. What a resource for the young man!
Undoubtedly, the older man instructed the boy on knowledge
vital to a fourteen-year-old, such as knifework and fishing. But
when they finally met in person, it wasn't a child but a
GROWN MAN! What a laugh they must have had! And to top
it all, the alleged "boy" DIDN'T EVEN FISH!

Nevertheless, it is often the anonymous users that come up with
the best ideas. User "ELECTROBALLS" (evidently an avid
sportsman) suggested that, in order to conserve paper, we
should be using acronyms for the most common sayings of our
time. For instance, if someone says something uproariously
humorous, it should be indicated by the letters "GA," for
"guffawing audibly." Even funnier passages should be rewarded
with "IJEMBAHNTWWTWM." (I just evacuated my bowels
and have no tissue with which to wipe myself!)

Yet there are other common sayings which aren't necessarily
humorous but are used in America so often, they warrant
truncation. Like "IAFWT." (I am afflicted with typhoid!) Or
"JPMW." (Just poisoned my wife!)

In fact, in an effort to force users to be more succinct, some
have suggested a new space limit on messages. Given that
nobody has an unlimited attention span, a 3,500 character limit
has   been   urged   on   transmissions.   User
"LIGHTNINGWEINER23" has argued that he has far too
many demands on his time to read long passages. He said just
the other day he was occupied for most of the day "binge-
watching" his children.

Others are worried that the network might devolve into a contest to see whose transmissions are most widely read. Rather than information egalitarianism, readership will be concentrated among those who appeal to the lowest common denominator.

For instance, user "LUV2BONE" has begun the practice of listing characteristics that contemporaneously make readers feel unique, yet also part of an underappreciated cognoscenti. The popularity of his most recent posting, "Ten Signs Your Mother Tried to Give You to the Well" narrowly eclipsed his previous post, "Twenty-three things only people who have lost an arm in a horrific heavy machinery accident at work and have no health insurance will understand." One would expect more from someone who is obviously a paleontologist!

January 8, 1916

In browsing through the various INTER-LOGS, I found one that fulfilled one of my desperate needs. In the listing, it was merely identified as "Tinder."

What a find! As it happens, I am always cold in my house, and never have enough firewood. Thus, any connection that can help me find an adequate reserve of affordable kindling is welcome indeed.

I went to this Tinder INTER-LOG and realized that I needed to set up a "profile" of some sort. It seemed odd that they needed personal information to sell me chopped up wood, but I obliged.

I informed potential sellers that I was a man who desperately needed warming up, and I would accept any man or woman that would help me in this mission! I sheepishly admit that, in order to get the best deal on firewood, I may have embellished my credentials slightly. I told them I was slightly taller and more muscular than I am and emphasized my preternatural endurance. Surely, the seller would keep the cost of kindling down if he wasn't forced to carry it back to my house for me!

It only took one day to get a response to my proposal. It was from a kind, elderly woman of 38 years old, who said she had more than I can handle! Intrigued, I set up a spot to rendezvous. But she picked the Spotted Clam saloon as the place we should meet, which struck me as queer as an eight-legged frog. Who had ever heard of such a thing? A woman in a saloon?

Yet I relented, and the date was made. The next night, I gathered two dollars in quarters and headed for the Spotted Clam, prepared to haul a good deal of firewood home. I entered the saloon and sat at the bar. After no more than ten minutes, I saw a matronly figure enter the bar, walking around in search of this fictional muscle-bound 6-foot-2 fellow. She was plain of face, gray of hair, and buck of tooth. As she glided through the bar, she resembled an otter searching for its final resting place.

She approached me and stood for a moment, staring directly at my face. Knowing who she was and why she was there, I spoke first.

"I'm sorry, I might not be as large as I said on the FINGER-PHONE, but I can assure you, I am more than adequate."

She shrugged, saying, "Oh, you'll do."

"Can you show me the wood?" I asked.

"Isn't that your job?" she responded.

I squinted my eyes and cocked my head sideways. An awkward silence enveloped us.

"Excuse me?"

She moved closer to me and put her hand on top of mine, which was resting on the bar. If this was her way of getting a better price out of me, it was absolutely not going to work!

"I only have two dollars, and that's all you're getting out of me!" I announced.

She seemed taken aback but didn't move. "Keep your money, young man," she whispered, as she got closer.

Before I knew it, I could feel the wiry hairs emanating from her chin brush my ear. Then, she touched me in a way that would have gotten her thrown out of the most disreputable cat house in Mexico!

"By the sideburns of Rasputin!" I cried, jumping back. "What chicanery is this, old woman?"

"I may not be much to look at," she answered, "but remember, in the dark, all cats are gray."

It was clear that this woman's intention was not, in fact, to sell me firewood of any kind. She was looking for a spark of the priapic variety, even at her advanced age!

I am keenly familiar with Benjamin Franklin's century-old theory that women age from the top down. "The Face first grows lank and wrinkled; then the Neck; then the Breast and Arms," Franklin once wrote, adding that "the lower Parts continuing to the last as plump as ever."

But this woman's attempt to take advantage of a man merely in need of a good fire in his home was an outrage. Perhaps I would just wear a sweater.

As I slowly backed out of the saloon, I left the two dollars on a table and said she could have it for her trouble. I had a mind to find the nearest policeman on the street to have him investigate her for the serious crime of misrepresentation of firewood, but I was running late. I had some knife-sharpening implements to go purchase from a young man I contacted on "Grinder."

You may be wondering, "Who is this fellow whose wisdom is being thrust into my home?"

An excellent question.

In my current position, I am a typist at the Milwaukee Post, the city's sixth-largest newspaper. (Currently behind the Milwaukee Journal, the Milwaukee Sentinel, the Social Democratic Herald, the Seebote German paper, and the Butter, Cheese, and Egg Journal.)

Our publication recently purchased five brand new, state of the art Linotype machines, which set the type for the paper. In the afternoon, a page from the newsroom rushes down the handwritten stories our reporters have penned and distributes them to my colleagues and me. We then type the stories, with each line of text being injected into a mold of molten lead, to be placed in a rack for the printer.

It is tedious work, to be sure. And often dangerous! If a letter sticks in the machine, the typist can often be subjected to molten lead being squirted upon his stomach or arms. Several colleagues have lost fingers among the hundreds of gears that keep the Linotype machine humming. To demonstrate his compassion, our employer will generally grant the typist the rest of the day off unpaid in the event the employee loses a digit or limb.

And while the job certainly doesn't pay a great deal, the chances of moving up the ladder at work are substantial. Our current typesetter, Basil Featherstone, only had to work the typing machines for sixteen years before his promotion to layout! Even small publications like ours are enormously profitable. As cities continue to grow, certainly daily newspapers will explode in popularity, as will their revenue. And surely, all of this largesse will flow to the workers that have helped build these infallible print empires!

It is also an influential profession. Newspaper typists bring news of the world to the populace, whether rich or poor. Sometimes, when we are typing out a reporter's handwritten story, we will catch errors, such as when a reporter "buries a lede." Although I have to admit, it took me several years to realize "lede" isn't spelled "lead." I actually once suggested a reporter write a story on why this is the case and only mention the main point at the end of the story.

In fact, in the 1850s, it was a group of Milwaukee Sentinel typists who sneaked into the company's headquarters late at night and changed the spelling of "Milwaukie" to "Milwaukee," thus settling a dispute over the spelling of the city's name that often prevented citizens from even speaking to one another!

Indeed, Milwaukee is a city close to my heart. My father, Franz, left Germany as a ten-year-old boy in 1870. In order to save him from the Franco-Prussian war, his parents nailed him into a barrel of beets and put him on a ship bound for America. Yet one of the deckhands, hungry for a delicious rooted vegetable, opened the barrel and found Franz hiding within.

When asked what he was doing there, my father answered, "I'm some beets." When the deckhand called a fellow shipmate for verification, they determined that he was not, in fact, a vegetable of any kind. Yet as soon as they turned away from him, he was able to stow away while doing a passable impersonation of a yam.

While in America, Franz was able to earn jobs doing hard labor on boats traveling throughout the Great Lakes. He was lucky, as the minimum age for dangerous work was eight. (Unions later succeeded in raising the age for life-threatening work to fourteen, given that young children were taking all of their jobs.) Soon, he found himself in Milwaukee, one of the fastest growing cities in America.

In little to no time, Franz was able to gain employment in one of the city's booming breweries. In order to pay off the debts of the Civil War, the federal government began imposing a one-dollar tax for every barrel of whiskey. This had the effect of doubling the cost of a glass of whiskey in saloons across America, thereby forcing more thirsty Americans into the arms of delicious, sudsy beer.

Shortly thereafter, in 1871, a great fire in the nearby city of Chicago crippled that city's breweries. Thus, Milwaukee, with its large German population, stepped in and became the nation's leader in beer production. Breweries such as Pabst, Schlitz, Miller, and Blatz almost doubled their production in the twelve months following the Chicago fire. The breweries, shrewd in their marketing and flush with money, would often pay for celebrities to walk into saloons and loudly announce, "I am drinking to the health of Milwaukee's greatest beer brewer, Captain Fred Pabst!" Imagine that. Buying a product because a famous person tells you to!

It was Americans' healthy interest in beer that allowed Franz to take a wife and spawn me, in 1889. I was fortunate to have been born in such a modern city. Between 1900 and 1910, the city's manufactured products doubled – prosperity rained money upon the city.

As a child, I was a dutiful but bored student. When asked to write a report about the great Civil War general Ambrose Burnside, for whom the facial hair known as "sideburns" are named, I demurred. Instead, I wrote about the lesser-known, but infinitely more interesting, General Alastair Soulpatch, who was fatally struck down by his own troops for refusing to cease playing his saxophone.

Even on his modest salary from the brewery, my father was able to pay for me to go to college at the new Marquette University, run by the Catholic Church's Jesuit congregation. Their rules were strict, although my behavior was often not in keeping with the Church's rigorous teachings of self-denial. My roommate and I would often stay up all night, enjoying Milwaukee's finest malted beverages. We likely kept several of the city's breweries afloat just by ourselves!

These late night sessions were generally rife with chicanery. My roommate, Boomer Mills, was a portly young fellow full of vigor, and quite the prankster. I awoke on more than one occasion with his derriere hovering above my head, attempting to break wind on me.

It was these gay hijinks that led me to leave the university after one year. It's not as though I left without gaining any knowledge. I initially took to the study of history; specifically, I enjoyed reading the stories of famous Europeans who toured America and wrote home with their observations of the unique American culture.

Naturally, it was the Frenchman Alexis de Tocqueville who became the most famous of these explorers – as his description of the American ethos was frighteningly spot on. In fact, de Tocqueville spent a good bit of time in my native Wisconsin. But I was particularly enamored with the German explorer Gerhardt Rodl, who endeavored to write the definitive account of America for his countrymen.

Rodl was mostly known for traveling the countryside and loudly exclaiming everything he saw. As he passed down America's bumpy roads, he would yell "Look, a sparrow!" or "Look, a grey squirrel!" or "Look, a river!" or "Look, a cow!" or "Look, clouds!" or "Look, trees!" This lasted for a little over two months before Rodl was bludgeoned to death by members of his traveling party. Sadly, the last entry of his journal reads, "I saw the most peculiar lizard today! And I said..."

Perhaps the most notable explorer of today is Joseph Meisner, who has taken to documenting America with moving pictures. Meisner has been visiting college towns and imploring female students to let him film their necklaces up close. What an inventive way to study the art of the locket! Imagine the untold educational possibilities that moving pictures hold.

My post-collegiate years also saw several attempts at starting businesses that never took flight. I tried writing a book called "Overcoming Dyslexia" that was written backward – it seemed penning it any other way would just be cruel. Sadly, I was not able to convince a book company to fund my endeavor. After that, I proposed a charity called "Lips of Love," which encouraged men to shave their moustaches off and mail them to sick children under the age of five that could not grow hair on their upper lip. Again, my idea was met with deafening indifference.

It was then that I saw an advertisement for a typesetter in the Milwaukee Post. Given that I knew the alphabet, and suspected that I could capably press a typewriter key that corresponded with each individual letter written on a page, I figured the job was made for me.

And it is thus that I became employed, made invaluable friends at the newspaper, and came into possession of the futuristic machine on which I am currently typing. Typically, the rule is once one obtains a FINGER-PHONE they are sworn to secrecy. But I admit, I have let several of my co-workers in on the fact that I own a social technology that is certain to transform the world.

Several of them have told me I should write a book as if I possessed a FINGER-PHONE a century ago. They thought it would be fascinating to explore how the world has changed since 1816 and thought I could make endless cheap jokes featuring historical anachronisms. But what sane person would read such dreck?

When I walked into work on Monday, word had spread that the German Kaiser had been infected with blood poisoning, and his predicament was dire. As I entered the story into the Linotype, I considered what effect these tiny infected blood cells could have on the world stage.

One never roots for someone to die. But if Germany's Kaiser were to expire, perhaps it would bring about the end of the savage war in Europe that some have taken to calling the "Great War." In fact, with millions of soldiers and civilians lying dead in its wake, there is certainly nothing "great" about the war. Would any man in his right mind take to calling an economic downturn a "great depression?" Inconceivable.

In fact, Wisconsin cheesemakers are among the few for whom the war is "great." With European cheese-producing countries like France gripped by conflict, cheese exports from this state have exploded in the prior two years. Last year, America produced thirty-two million pounds of cheese – half of it manufactured in Wisconsin!

President Woodrow Wilson has been coy about whether to get the United States involved in the savagery abroad. And with an election coming up this year, he maintains that none of our American boys will die in the trenches in France. But the world has recently seen such acts of evil that our involvement seems inevitable. I say we not only need to end the war, America needs to punish Germany for famous events such as the Torpedoing of the Lusitania, the Rape of Belgium, and the Relative Discomfort of Strasbourg.

Clearly infallible sources within British intelligence have discovered that the German Army has been taking the bodies of dead British soldiers and sending them to a fat rendering plant to be turned into candles! It is rumored that one British officer's widow, upon getting remarried, actually received her old husband as a gift. (He had been renamed "Coastal Breeze.")

Needless to say, the war against the Kaiser is not as popular in a city with such a Germanic heritage. After editorializing in favor of preparedness for war, our paper often receives bitter letters from German citizens accusing the Post of being in the pocket of war profiteers. More than one letter has reached the Post accusing the paper of being in the employ of British newspaper magnate Lord Northcliffe, who has rallied the British public in opposition to the Kaiser.

Such strong feelings have aroused suspicion about the city's immigrant populations. In a speech last week, one university professor condemned so-called "hyphenated Americans," saying, "American citizenship permits no divided loyalty, and those who conspire against the peace and honor of this country are engaged in acts that are wicked and dangerous." This has only added to the dislike of recently arrived Italians, Germans, Irish and Poles, who are seen as taking the jobs of Americans and breeding indiscriminately.

But Germans have especially been singled out for venomous attacks, given the Kaiser's butchery in Europe. One of our paper's reporters went out on the street and asked passersby what they thought should be done to the Kaiser once captured. One woman said he should be handed over to the prettiest girls in Belgium, who would pull his moustache hairs out one at a time!

City resident Frank Falkner told a reporter that Kaiser Wilhelm should be dressed in a pneumatic suit and thrown from the roof of the Wisconsin Hotel "and then let him bounce until he starved to death." What an oddly specific, and thus disquieting, suggestion! Clearly, Frank Falkner was walking around the city waiting for a reporter to ask him this very question.

January 10, 1916

On my walk to work today, I passed what's known as the "artist's neighborhood," where Bohemians thrive. The street is lined with shops selling artisanal products that I have never actually witnessed anyone purchasing. The men, often actors, poets, or musicians, either wear beards reminiscent of Europe or ironically shave their moustaches clean off. On some days, I have passed the occasional young man whose odor is so foul, he was most certainly counted four times in the most recent census!

To prove their authenticity, these Bohemians enjoy fashion and hobbies of an earlier time; many dress in the garb of the 1860s. On the corner, two young Bohemians were listing their top five Percy Bysshe Shelley poems, when one defiantly declared that he "liked a lot of his earlier stuff" and that "everything after 'To a Skylark' insists too much upon itself."

As I walked closer to my office, I passed the spot where former president Teddy Roosevelt was shot just a few years ago. Roosevelt was actually saved from the assassin's bullet by the lengthy speech he had written out and placed in his breast pocket, which slowed the projectile enough for him to go on speaking for another hour. This led one onlooker to sneer that our dear Teddy was only "half-shot." It seems as though, had he not been such a gaseous windbag, his fifty-page written speech would have been thinner and he wouldn't be alive today!

In fact, it appears the years following his presidency have been tough for old TR. After his eight years in the White House ended in 1908, he grew displeased with the conservatism of Republican candidate William Howard Taft in 1912 and decided to run again as a third-party Progressive candidate. TR only received 24% of the vote, but likely stole votes from Taft, allowing Democrat Woodrow Wilson to ascend to the presidency with only 42% of the vote.

This has rightfully earned Roosevelt the enmity of the more conservative members of the Republican Party, who blame TR for foisting the decidedly left-wing Wilson upon the world. They also believe Roosevelt may make another presidential run, this time as a member of the Bull Moose Party, but this seems far-fetched. Surely Republicans have now learned not to allow their party to be overtaken by a small group of ideological extremists.

As I made my way into the Milwaukee Post, I was greeted by my old friend Ned at the front door. Ned keeps a loaded revolver in the drawer at his desk, as he is frequently confronted by citizens upset about what has been printed about them in the newspaper. One day, a local inebriate rushed into the office yelping that there was an elephant seen running around a local cemetery. Ned quickly subdued the raving lunatic, dragged him out the front door, and bid him adieu with a firm foot to the posterior. The next day, the headline in the Milwaukee Journal read, "Elephant Found in Local Cemetery." The story was absolutely true!

I walked downstairs to begin my day of typing up the stories that had been sent down to us from the night before. In our business, speed is paramount – readers absolutely must be able to read the news within three days of an event happening or it is considered moot.

All of our Linotype machines are kept in the basement and set in a row in a cramped cinderblock room. Half the room is set aside for the racks where the letters are arranged for the printing press. Reporters, of course, are held in much higher regard, and therefore inhabit the upper levels of the building, which have windows and views of the city's downtown. The view has been diminished somewhat, however, as fencing has been placed over the windows to discourage people on the street throwing bombs into the newsroom.

You won't hear any argument from me that our reporters don't deserve the high standing granted them by our paper's ownership. Many of them are true professionals that know all the tricks of the trade. One of our paper's best reporters, Dirk Calloway, has learned how to break bad news to families in exchange for details about their deceased loved ones. Once, Calloway was found drinking heavily in a house of ill repute. When the police barged in, he began yelling at the officers, telling them he was working on a secret investigative series and they had just blown his cover. After the police apologized and let him go, he admitted to the newsroom that he merely had been investigating the contents of a buxom redhead's blouse!

My dearest friend in the typesetting room, however, is young Philetus Liptrot, a thick, blunt twenty-three-year-old who is confident he can see into the future. "Philly," as he has come to be known, was recently reading about women in Europe who have actually had substances like beeswax injected into their bosoms to enhance their size! Imagine. Young Philly has a theory that one day the facial reconstruction surgery being used on the wounded soldiers in Europe will be utilized to benefit vain upper-class women who simply want to improve their looks.

"You watch," he told me one morning. "There will be a day when we won't be able to tell the old from adolescents. Elderly men will dress in the clothing of their youth. Women, thinking they are eternally young, will read books meant for their daughters. The respect paid to society's elderly will disappear, as they will be indistinguishable from school-aged boys and girls." He is certain that at some point we will see young people dropping dead in the street, only to find out they were actually in their 80s! A preposterous idea!

Typing up the scraps of news this week involved a great deal of drudgery, as the first week of the year is typically slow. "Leap Year Maids Seek Gay Bachelors," read the headline of my first piece, which essentially read as a tribute to an aspiring young actress seeking a new beau. It actually contained the following acrid bit of poetry, intended to lure some poor bachelor into her honeyed trap. The emetic poem, with the novel title of "Love," read as follows:

"L says I'm lonesome, as lonesome as can be;

O says you're old, but that don't worry me;

V whispers virtue, you want in your wife;

E stands for every happy day of your life (if you marry me!)"

It is rumored that the great Wordsworth has emerged from his

grave with the intention of murdering this woman for her crime
against decent vers libre!

As I read the article aloud, Philly chimed in, saying he had just
seen a woman wearing a shoulder-baring dress the previous
evening. I asked who this delectable young woman was.

"Oh, it was some sad old broad I saw standing by herself at the
Spotted Oyster."

When I walked into work the next day, further flimflammery
was afoot! As I strode through the basement door, I noticed the
most pungent of odors. The room smelled of musty perfume, as
if a gaggle of suffragist shrews had come to nag us all.

I immediately saw young Philly and loudly asked him if, given
the smell, he had spent the evening in one of the city's low-end
brothels – the kind that accepts payment in tobacco. Expecting
laughter, I instead received a look of horror on the young man's
face! Without speaking, he lifted his finger and began pointing
to my right. I slowly turned and looked past the first row of
typing machines. There, at the very end, I saw what had caused
poor Philly to look as if he had seen an apparition.

Sitting on the last stool, typing like a hummingbird, was...A
WOMAN.

She appeared to be a young lady in her early twenties, with fair
skin and light brown hair. Without her fingers ever stopping,
she looked at me briefly, smiled, and said "Hello." She then
turned back and continued typing.

For this, I could not stand! "Great Christ!" I ejaculated. "They
are trying to ruin us!"

I turned to my coworker Otto to ask what had happened. "Paper hired her yesterday," he said.

"This is inconceivable!" I quite appropriately protested.

I immediately bolted up to the main office to complain to management about this attack on workplace comity.

"Who is that viperess in the typing office?" I asked Harold Ellis, the office manager. He said her name was Virginia, and she was the daughter of a large shareholder in the paper.

"Don't worry," he said. "She's making thirty percent of what you men are making."

I told him that salary was outrageous, as it is well above the three percent of men's salary that women typically make!

"How are we supposed to function with a lady in the room?" I demanded to know. "What if we begin talking about politics, or world affairs, or philosophy, or sports? She will be LOST. What if someone is telling really good jokes and she doesn't understand any of them? What if she is powdering her nose and instead of typing 'President Decries War,' she types, 'President Declares War,' leading Germany to attack America and lay waste to this great nation, leaving humans feeding on each other for sustenance whilst living amongst its burning ruins?"

He told me to return to work.

January 15, 1916

I have been subjected to the most insidious calumny!

After starting up my FINGER-PHONE yesterday, I left to pour myself a delicious glass of milk. Upon returning from obtaining my dairy treat, my FINGER-PHONE had printed out a missive so vile I am not sure I can repeat it.

It appears another chap going by the nom de plume "BOOTYCRUSHR" had read my posting from last week and took quite the issue with my characterization of Teddy Roosevelt. I can only presume this angry FINGER-PHONE user reads from the Progressive hymnal and was therefore unimpressed by my declaring TR to be a "gaseous windbag."

The poisonous communique read:

> Dear fellow FINGER-PHONE user:
>
> I found your insulting description of the great President Roosevelt to be juvenile and mean-spirited. It is a window into the soul of someone who is hopelessly corrupt!
>
> Further, I have found your writing to be tedious and turgid. If whoever invented the sentence was still alive, he would sue you for copyright infringement if he knew what you were doing to his good name! Indeed, if any portion of

your INTERLOG post were to be read aloud at a funeral, the corpse would jump from the casket and try to strangle the reader!

What you have done to the English language, and humanity itself, has made me lachrymose. The only benefit your writings could possibly yield would be to be spread them over a field as fertilizer in order to feed a starving African village.

I would wager handsomely that you don't have the gumption to respond to this!

This breach of comity will not stand! I intend to write a detailed retort to this Cro-Magnon to set him straight. If the FINGER-PHONE network of users is good for anything, it is for being able to craft reasonable, well-thought-out responses to such attacks. Undoubtedly, other users within the club, wherever they may be, are home writing their denunciations of this thickheaded baboon as I sit here typing.

But as you, dear reader, know, it was a busy week at the Post, full of important news.

At the end of last week, a committee within the United States Senate favorably reported a constitutional amendment allowing women's suffrage to the full Senate. It is known as the "Susan B. Anthony Amendment," and it would end the ability of states to deny suffrage to females.

Coincidentally, on Monday, there was a meeting held down at the public library to educate the city's residents on women's suffrage. I was taken aback a bit when young Philly asked me to attend the informational meeting, as he is not known around the office as being a staunch supporter of the National Women's Party.

I myself am skeptical that the fairer sex will ever be able to vote. A half a century ago, black Americans were granted the franchise, but strong evidence exists that catastrophe will ensue if the "irresponsible vote" were doubled for ladies.

Nonetheless, these women are insistent! While some complain about the influence of business groups on public policy, these well-heeled interests have nowhere near the coercive power as a wife that has her mind made up! As Blaise Pascal once said, the entire world would be different if Cleopatra had a slightly shorter nose.

In fact, a recently released study showed definitively that if women were allowed to show up and cast votes, those polling places are six times more likely to be attacked by a swarm of bees! It is rumored that in Virginia last year, a group of lady protesters tried to dress as men and vote, and a fleet of yellow jackets descended upon the voting booths, stinging sixteen people and casting thirty-five ballots themselves. Who are we, as humans, to defy the natural scientific order?

It is not as though men haven't sacrificed enough for women. In our city, ladies have been complaining incessantly about a man's God-given right to spit tobacco juice wherever he pleases. Women's groups claimed that the juice was ruining their dresses as they dragged along the city's sidewalks. But the husbands have argued quite reasonably that tobacco juice keeps moths away!

Nevertheless, the city's women have sought retribution by loudly ringing bells in the ears of any man caught expectorating the contents of his mouth in public. Needless to say, this endless nagging has not endeared them to the town's menfolk; although, instead of chewing tobacco, many have shifted their habits to the much healthier practice of smoking cigarettes.

In fact, if women ever do earn the franchise, it will be solely because men cannot take the constant badgering anymore. Last year, an English lady suffragette named Emily Davison threw herself in front of King George's horse at the Epsom Derby, killing herself in the name of voting rights. This is outrageous – imagine the psychological counseling the horse needed afterward.

It is not as if the public has not had its say on the matter. Who can forget the 1912 public referendum on women's suffrage that failed by a 2-to-1 margin? Everyone knows that once wives can vote, American men will be denied the opportunity to enjoy beer with their cronies. The fact that eligible voters rejected the female vote 63% to 37% is proof positive that 100% of individuals don't want women voting.

So I asked young Philly why he wanted to attend this meeting, given that it appears his mind is pretty well made up. He looked at me and simply said "Trim," before cackling maniacally. It is evident I must keep up with the fast-changing nomenclature of what we call "Generation A." And I am only four years older than this ruffian!

Nevertheless, when the shift whistle blew, off we trudged in the cold air on our way to the library. Typically, these detours on the way home from work would find us in a local saloon. But it seemed to me merely attending this suffrage meeting would look good to any prospective woman who would have me. And the appearance of having an open-minded beau is much less expensive than a bouquet of flowers!

Philly and I took our seats before Miss Ada James, chairwoman of the Women's Suffrage Association, began to speak. As she laid out her weak arguments – that women make up more than half the population, that they are full citizens, that they, too, pay taxes for government services – Philly grew visibly restless.

Then, without warning, young Philly covered his mouth and yelled "RUG MUNCHER!"

What a queer thing to say! As the twenty-five heads in the crowd swiveled around to see who was responsible for the verbal ejaculation, I immediately looked at the floor. As it happens, there was nobody attempting to ingest the carpet in the library. I was certainly fond of the pattern, but I wasn't particularly hungry.

As the meeting resumed, Philly could take no more. He immediately stood up and bolted via the back door. It was a fairly abrupt exit, as he never even got the chance to "trim" whatever he came after. As far as I could tell, he didn't even bring any scissors with him.

The next day, my first typing assignment brought news of the important 1916 presidential race. The primary candidate mentioned in Republican circles is Supreme Court Justice Charles Evans Hughes. But Hughes' candidacy brings special challenges; as a member of the nation's high court, he is not allowed to say anything about his positions on public policy matters. It perhaps does not portend well that at a recent speaking engagement, when asked about the new national income tax, Justice Hughes pointed and yelled, "Look over there, an otter playing the violin!" before pulling a burlap sack over his head and sprinting from the room.

If Justice Hughes is considering running, he has plenty of time to decide. Who would ever begin a presidential campaign in January? As I have often said, politicians are like chilled sides of beef; the longer they are subjected to sunlight, the acrider they smell. Surely, Republicans have many months to groom a suitable challenger to the Democrat Wilson, who has never enjoyed the support of the majority of Americans.

Yet one challenge for the Republicans is that while Wilson won in 1912 with meager support it was largely because so many voted for TR on the Progressive ticket. When added together, nearly 80 percent of Americans eschewed stalwart Republicanism – it is almost as if the more conservative wing of the Grand Old Party has received a Jack Johnson left hook!

The Progressives know this and thus are trying to draft the ol' Rough Rider back into service this year. At their annual meeting this week in Chicago, the Progressive Party debated whether to re-incorporate itself with its former counterparts in the Republican Party. In this sense, they are holding a pistol to the heads of the Grand Old Party; either the party adopts a Progressive platform and the Progressives rejoin the party, or the Progressives remain their own party and send the Republican presidential candidate into what is surely a suicide mission in 1916. It seems very much the case of the organ grinder taking instructions from his monkey!

I admit to not following politics as closely as I should – despite my job of typing the news for public consumption. Until recently, candidates won primarily on their service in America's

Civil War, not on the policy positions they held. Once, a group
of state legislators was brought to our building to discuss an
issue with our editorial board. While there were four legislators
present, I counted only eleven limbs among them. Generally,
the more arms and legs you had lost in the battle with the
South, the more electable you became. There is a rumor that
one state legislator served for forty years with a wooden head!

Yet a much more pressing matter for Americans is that of
Mexico. As you recall, last week, an army employed by the
bandit Pancho Villa attacked a train in Chihuahua City,
Mexico, killing seventeen Americans. It is up to President
Wilson to decide how to respond to this butchery, as it appears
the United States has now been drawn into a civil war to the
south.

I certainly am no military strategist, but it would seem to be
folly to engage the strength of the U.S. military in Mexico while
also preparing for the possibility of joining the war in Europe. It
seems as if there is little near the border there to defend,
anyway. According to press reports, America has just added the
states called "Arizona" and "New Mexico" to the union, but
these rumors are sparsely sourced. If the bandit Villa was to
invade America, he would likely do so in either of these alleged
states – would we really miss them all that much?

More importantly, it is not immigration by Mexicans about
which Uncle Sam should stay up all night worrying. Hungarian
statesman Gyula De Pekar gave a speech last week in which he
declared that because of "hyphenated Americans" America has
"ceased to be a nation." De Pekar deemed the extent to which
new immigrants cling to their native cultures to be "popular
indigestion."

President Wilson has already addressed the issue of immigration, saying last May that you "cannot dedicate yourself to America unless you become in every respect, and with every purpose of your will, thoroughly Americans."

"A man who thinks of himself as belonging to a particular national group in America has not yet become an American; and the man who goes among you to trade upon your nationality is no worthy son to live under the Stars and Stripes!" said Wilson.

Thus, it appears President Wilson may actually agree with De Pekar on the issue of immigrant assimilation. Perhaps the Hungarian De Pekar indeed has the color and shape of America all figured out. Just imagine a century from now when it is the dream of all the world's citizens to live in the utopia of Hungary!

January 29, 1916

Upon sending my detailed retort to my learned progressive friend several weeks ago, I waited days for a response. I then re-sent the same communication with an additional note saying "I just wanted to make sure you saw this." Still, I received no reply. It is almost as if the anonymous individual at the other end of the communication knows that going dark is making me more anxious than anything he could possibly write! Is he winning merely by causing me to waste my time worrying about him?

When I woke on Thursday, however, there appeared to be a message from him on my FINGER-PHONE. Yet it was a very cryptic one, in keeping with the most hallowed secret societies of Europe. It was one line that simply read:

8==D~ ~

What could this mean? Clearly, he meant it as a clue to some larger truth he was trying to convey! Perhaps it was an invitation to join a prestigious fraternal organization; it did somewhat look like a key – but to unlock what?

That day, I set out to decipher this message. I took the typed page from the FINGER-PHONE and jammed it into my pocket before heading to work. I knew someone in the city would know what the series of characters meant; so I began pulling it from my jacket and showing it to people on the street during my walk to the office. I presumed if it were an invitation to a secret society, the individual who recognized it wouldn't want me to give away the code. Thus, when I showed it to strangers, I made sure to accompany it with the wink of an eye so as not to give away the secret!

I was somewhat surprised by the revulsion showed by many of those I questioned. An elderly woman even attempted to hit me with her cane and yelled for the police! One young man I encountered said, "Okay, but that will be one dollar. Go pay the man around the corner." I refused – wondering why I would have to pay someone else to view my secret code.

It was then that I realized I may have stumbled upon something far deeper than I had envisioned. I declared that I would find out exactly what this code meant – but later, as I was tardy for work!

When I got to the office, my dear friend, and typesetter extraordinaire, Basil Featherstone approached me to see if I would be interested in joining him next month at a performance at the old Wilmont Theater.

Normally, I try to avoid crowded theaters, as I often fear for my safety while taking in a show. They have gotten much safer, however – according to recent statistics, one now only has a seven percent chance of being burned alive while enjoying a performance. The Wilmont, funded by local brewing millionaire Ernst Schilke, burned down in 1890, only to be rebuilt one year later on the same site. When that theater burned down, it was rebuilt once again. Of course, that theater was also taken to the ground by the Devil's tongue. It is rumored that when the architect drew up the blueprints for the next theater, those spontaneously combusted in his hands!

But I decided to attend because my bond with Basil is so strong. He is a tall man with thick black hair and an impeccably manicured moustache. He is also an immaculate dresser; even while placing the cast letters into the printing frames, he has nary a blot of ink on him. His knowledge of the European theater is second to none; rarely does a day go by that he doesn't dazzle us with a brilliant quote from Oscar Wilde. He has never divulged his age, but a trained eye would put him at about thirty-seven years without ever having been married - what young maiden in her right mind wouldn't have snapped him up yet? What a fine husband he will make!

I told Basil to go ahead and purchase the tickets, on the assumption that the theater would be there by the time the show came around. Evidently, it was a musical performance by a much talked about singer from Minneapolis whose latest song is entitled, "I Want 2 Show my Pantaloons 2 U." I told Featherstone that it would be a much gayer time if he were to bring a lady friend, as well. He chuckled, pursed his lips, and said, "I doubt that."

As the work whistle blew that evening, young Philly joined Basil and me for a drink down at the XX Saloon, mere blocks away from the Post. I had my traditional glass of Duffy's Pure Malt Whiskey. Basil told me it was ironic that I asked for a "healthy pour," as the amount of whiskey in my glass would most likely kill me. Clearly, he hasn't seen the newspaper advertisements, in which doctors all over America recommend Duffy's restorative as an antidote to the common cold, aches and pains, and nagging wives!

Medicinal benefits aside, alcohol is the very foundation of fraternal companionship. As local scribe Gunnar Mickleson recently editorialized, "Beer and wine make for conversation. There is in liquors of mild alcoholic persuasion that which quickens the flow of the thoughts in a man's cranium, loosens a notch the belt about his reticence, and releases upon his tongue the fruits of his meditations. It is for precisely this reason that men have resorted to alcoholic drinks as a means to make their companionship more vivid and happy."

Curse those who would deny us of this right! It is only the toxic alliance of progressives and wives that would commit such evil.

As the night went on, Basil, sipping on a Bordeaux, waxed extensively about the advantages of youth that he no longer enjoys. "When you're a young man, you imbibe to create new memories," he said, looking at the ceiling. "When you are old, you drink to forget things."

Later in the evening, Philly abruptly announced that he had to leave. It seems that Mrs. Valenti, the wife of prominent Milwaukee attorney Emil Valenti, was all alone while her husband was away on business. What a sport of Philly to go cheer her up in her time of distress. I was so taken by his philanthropy, I offered to join him. "No thanks," he said, abruptly holding his hand up.

Still, how thoughtful of him to comfort her in this time of loneliness. Perhaps he will even entertain her young son, who was born while her husband was on a two-year trade mission to the Orient.

As I stumbled home, I made a short detour into a small grocer to purchase some cigarette papers. It is owned by a local Jewish family, and the familiar face of their teenaged daughter Golda was working the cash register; she said she was trying to save up enough money to return to teaching school. I tossed her an extra dime and ordered her not to forget my good deed when she was famous someday!

February 2, 1916

President Wilson continues to be sharply criticized for remaining neutral in the War in Europe. Pacifists such as La Follette see Wilson's continued neutrality as a sign he will eventually renege on his promise to keep America off the European shores. Others, such as Teddy Roosevelt, are stridently pro-war and believe Wilson is only remaining neutral so he can be re-elected this year. But who would make such a decision based on politics?

The third group, however, are Wilson supporters that believe preparedness is the moderate alternative. Oddly, many of Wilson's most ardent conservative critics fall into this category. Quite often, stalwart Republicans take to the floor of Congress to urge support of a man they would otherwise throw off the dome of the Capitol building.

But those urging immediate action to aid Britain and France have good reason to advocate for American introduction into the war. Recently, the Deutsche Tageszeitungen printed another German "Hymn of Hate" directed at England. Composed by Georg von Kries, the lyrics are as follows:

> We warm ourselves with internal anger, we warm ourselves
> with rage, for outside our walls there is loud rejoicing, and

many a golden palace is being built on false victories.

The thunder of our cannon – which is the German tempest – penetrates thick walls and reaches us in our dungeon. We clench our fists savagely and wish we were there. We lie here like beggars in the frost, with open doors. We may not fight for Germany, we only starve for her.

May every bomb hit you, accursed England, till London's factories are in ashes, and her palatial banks are mere heaps of ruins! Each bomb will have said to you: "So we hated you!"

And if the bombs fell on us, we should not complain, for that would mean an end to our torments, and would be preferable to an English court of law.

The others are dying in battle and their blood flows gloriously, while we are dying, without honor, of misery, hate and rage.

The hymn is sung to the tune of "Skip to My Lou."

On Monday, the United States Supreme Court upheld the federal income tax, which was passed into law little more than two years ago. Some wealthy representatives of the Union Pacific Railroad had sued to avoid imposing the tax on its employees, but the Court rejected their argument, deeming both the law and its reciprocity constitutional.

Fortunately, I have no need to worry about the income tax. For one, the tax only applies to incomes of over $4,000 per year. I can only dream of such opulence! Further, my boss frequently uses it as a selling point for not raising my salary. "If I gave you a raise, Sebastian," he always says, "you would simply just be giving the excess funds to the government." So, I most earnestly thank him for allowing me to keep the money I earn.

Wednesday found me listening to the incessant whining of my fellow worker Otto Kleiner, who, at the advanced age of forty-six years, is still working in the Post typing office. Kleiner maintains that he is prematurely balding, which seems odd, given his many years. While I generally abhor the laws passed by Congress, I would accept one that declared the maximum age a man could say he was "prematurely balding." One would think thirty years old has to be the maximum!

Otto believes it is his hats that are denying him a sufficiently hirsute dome. Maybe it is his constant cigar smoking, poor diet, or his generally cantankerous attitude. But he is seen as an important asset to the newspaper, as he is the only employee of the typist room who actually writes copy for the paper itself.

Otto's primary duty is to answer the slate of reader letters the newspaper receives on a daily basis. Every now and then, the Post will get a letter that needs to be answered by the omniscient reporter class upstairs, but, for the most part, communications are random, insipid queries about worldly facts.

Seeing as how a robust set of Encyclopedia Britannica or even a basic almanac is too much of an extravagance for a regular American home, most readers just want information about the world outside their homes. Often times, children will write to the paper for relationship advice, thinking they are getting answers from a matronly expert on manners – not a portly, oleaginous misanthrope who spends more time scratching himself than typing responses.

Perhaps the newspaper's editors view the Post's readership as thoughtful, intelligent consumers of news that hang on every inked letter of the publication. But a sampling of letters suggests otherwise.

For example, the following letter was received yesterday:

To the Editor of the Post:

1. Who is more popular, the blonde or brunette?

2. What do brown and blue eyes signify?

3. How should a girl of 12 wear her hair?

4. I am 12 and in the seventh grade. Am I far enough advanced?

5. Is it proper for girls of 12 to go to shows at night?

6. Is the war almost at an end?

7. Should I give my teacher a Christmas present?

E.L.F.

Otto's answers:

1. Both have their admirers.

2. Brown: affectionate disposition, fondness of clothes. Blue: coquetry, fondness for fun.

3. Braided in one or two braids and tied with neat bows of ribbon.

4. Yes.

5. We do not think so.

6. We do not know.

7. You may do so if you wish.

This pattern is typical of both children and adults. Postage is expensive, so often times the inquisitor will combine the most disparate of topics into their list of questions, hoping to get it all on one page! Take, for example:

> 1. How can I become more acquainted with the young man with whom I think I am in love? 2. What is the proper way of entertaining a young man the first time he calls? 3. Give me a recipe for potato salad. 4. How is my handwriting?

Or this, from January 8:

> To the Editor of the Post: 1. Give me the number of square miles of England, Ireland, Scotland and Wales combined. 2. Of Illinois. 3. What is the population of Milwaukee at present? 4. How does a snake brush his teeth?

Earlier in the month, "I.M." wrote to the Post asking what games would be appropriate for guests between the ages of fifteen and twenty-one to play at a Leap Year party at their home. Otto suggested a game called "Lottery," where the males and females are separated and each pick paper numbers from a bowl.

The female is then paired up with the male with the same number, and for five minutes, the gender roles are switched, with men "performing tasks suitable to women," like embroidering, and women doing men's tasks, like "hammering nails." Then ice cream is served!

The other day, someone wrote asking whether a foreign person who becomes naturalized as a U.S. citizen could become president. Otto's answer, of course, was "No." In fact, any person running for office born in a faraway land occupied by savages – Hawaii, for instance – should be viewed with great suspicion. It shall be ever thus!

While America's status as the world's melting pot is admirable, the prohibition of non-Americans from holding the office of president is a sound one. Imagine if a man were to be born abroad and move here with their parents at the age of three. He moves his way up the political ladder, being elected to any number of offices on his journey to the presidency, all the while passing legislation and taking positions that are popular with voters. Then, once he becomes president, he forcibly seizes control of both houses of Congress and the Supreme Court and rules as a tyrant until the next presidential election. All because at the age of three he was indoctrinated into a fringe nationalistic group in his native land! We cannot be too cautious!

Presidential politics was also the topic du jour as the conservative Tory wing of the Republican Party met this week to try to reclaim the soul of their party from the progressives. The keynote speaker at their convention was noted female author Bess Morgan, who has written several bestselling books, with incendiary one-word titles like HORNSWAGGLED!, TREACHERY!, and IGNOMINY!, to cast aspersions against the political left.

Miss Morgan, a thin blonde, is primarily known for her outrageous attacks against progressives which often garner her substantial media coverage. At different times, she has accused progressive President Wilson of fathering a mulatto child out of wedlock, of often taking comfort in the arms of other men, and of being a robot! All of which, if they were true, would seem to be contradictory. (Attempts by reporters to contact Wilson's homosexual half-black robot baby have been unsuccessful.)

I have, however, "buried the lede," as we say in the news business. Our robot president is coming to town!

February 5, 1916

With Philly's help, I have discerned the meaning of the secret code. Let us not speak of it again.

(Also, if any fellow FINGER-PHONE users have devised a way – call it an "application" – to burn any posts previously typed out on another user's machine, please DISCREETLY MESSAGE me.)

Otherwise, it has been a singularly uncommon week!

On Monday morning, I frantically choked down some oatmeal, then gathered my jacket and hat before rushing out to see President Wilson speak at the Milwaukee Auditorium. I was reasonably haggard, as I worked late on Sunday night in order to get an hour off to go see the president on Monday.

Before I went to see the president speak, I stopped by the office to pick up a newspaper credential in order to gain entry to the venue. In the five minutes I was actually in the office, I noticed Philly chuckling at a bit of news that came across his typing station. In Geneva, Switzerland, eighteen train cars pulled up to the station, and every car was full of one-legged men returning to Germany from the war. (Ironically, the term for "greatly wounded" in French is "grands blesses!")

Philly wondered aloud whether a man should be charged less to ride the train if he is missing a leg. "He weighs less, and therefore less coal is needed to power the train because of his presence on it," he said aloud, to no one in particular. Philly said he, too, often took weight into consideration. "Although my personal motto," he said loudly while pointing at his moustache, "is fatties ride free."

While Philly's declaration seemed to have some sort of ribald undertone - as evidenced by Basil's rolling of the eyes - I was too far out the door to query him further.

As I approached the auditorium, a throng had developed outside in the streets. The Milwaukee Auditorium seats 7,000 men, and at least that many souls were outside the theater. Our paper's story would later report that over 20,000 people crammed downtown in hopes of seeing the president. One wonders how many people were there to see Wilson and how many were just drawn to the streets to see what the giant crowds were all about.

It was twenty degrees outside, but the mass of bodies made it warmer. The winter had been particularly brutal, and a quick look at the crowd showed the damage a typical Wisconsin winter will do; scattered among the throng were men with half-ears that had been mangled by frostbite.

I worked my way through the beehive to the entrance for newspaper reporters. Upon flashing my credential, I made my way to the section reserved for the press. We were pressed together so close, I could tell some reporters were incredibly excited about seeing President Wilson. Where else will anyone get the chance to see the man fully animated and speaking his mind? What if he were to make an announcement about the War in Europe that resonated throughout the world?

For about an hour, the crowd was treated to entertainment before the president and first lady arrived. At one point, the barbershop quartet Jake and the Smokestacks performed an old saloon favorite about a man who, on his wedding night, realizes his new wife has a wooden leg. Indeed, who can forget the lyrics to "I Married Half a Woman, Half a Tree?"

Behind Wilson were seated rows of individuals of varying nationalities, presumably to signal that the president had support from all Americans, no matter what their origin. But the obviousness of the ploy was worthy of a hearty roll of the eyes.

Sitting in the same proximity was an Indian woman, a Jewish rabbi, a Mexican laborer, and a black child. Perhaps Wilson's managers should have just gone the whole way with the charade and added a curly-moustached Italian man in a chef hat throwing pizza dough in the air, or a German wearing lederhosen while munching on a hearty bratwurst. The theatrical rainbow wouldn't be entirely complete without including a stereotype of every known nationality!

Before Wilson began his speech, he made his way within mere feet of the press area. He walked slowly, and his face was serious and eyes sallow.

When Wilson appeared on stage, his wires imperceptible, the boisterous crowd wailed its approval. But as the president began to speak, the cheers died down into a quiet reverence.

Yet soon, the quiet was likely more the result of confusion than respect. No human has ever uttered more words that, when combined, mean less than what Wilson said on that day. Every syllable from his mouth was sacrificed to the gods of equivocation. His speech was a verbal salad – while it took a good bit of time to eat, you realize minutes later that you're hungry again.

"I want at the outset to remove any misapprehension in your minds," Wilson began, before placing more misapprehension in the crowd's minds. "There is no crisis; nothing new has happened."

"We should see that our house is set in order. When all the world is afire, the sparks fly everywhere. America has drawn her blood and her energy out of almost all of the nations of the world," Wilson continued, adding, "We know that our roots and our traditions run best into other soils."

At that point, Murray Alexander, a photographer from the Milwaukee Sentinel, turned to me and asked, "Okay, so... are we going to war or not? I have a family hunting trip planned in the fall."

"I have not supposed that the men whose voices seemed to show a threat against us represented even the people that claimed to represent," Wilson continued. "I know the magic of America. I know the impulses which draw men to our shores. I know that they came to be free. I know that when the test comes every man's heart will be first for America," he declared to loud applause.

"There is daily, hourly danger that the nations absorbed in war will feel constrained to do things which are absolutely inconsistent with the rights of the United States," Wilson said, as he reached a crescendo. "They are not thinking of us; they are thinking first of all of their own affairs."

"I pledge you," Wilson finished, solemnly, "that, God helping, I will keep America out of war."

Wilson has repeatedly made this pledge before; some have charged that it is merely a ploy to gain re-election this year before committing U.S. troops to Europe. This idea was given credence on Monday with Wilson's invocation of the "God helping" loophole, which, evidently, would send the nation to war if God took some time off from helping to eat a sardine sandwich.

Imagine your wife asking you if you love her. And instead of answering "Yes" or "No," you begin a long speech about the great love affairs of history, what "love" has meant to different people over the course of time, and that you think you may be able to love her, "God helping." It would seem your wife would then clarify your feelings by striking a plate against the side of your head!

Nonetheless, the crowd, perhaps honored by the presence of the world's most important man in their midst, cheered wildly. At the moment, the attendees thought President Wilson was the ultimate statesman. But are we never to avenge the sinking of the Lusitania, which killed nearly two hundred Americans? It made me hope that someone would one day invent sliced bread so we had something better than Wilson with which to compare great things.

One entity not buying Wilson's pledge is the life insurance industry, which this week began adding war riders to their accident policies. Anyone signing up for a new life insurance policy as of this week will not receive any insurance money if they are killed "during the continuance of war in Europe, Asia, and Africa."

It is always interesting that the most accurate predictions of what will happen in the future come from groups with a vested financial interest in the outcome. This is why political writers and speechmakers are often so far off the mark! Perhaps Congress should implement a system by which every newsman that talks about politics must pay a fee. If his prediction is wrong, he loses the money forever. If his prediction is right, the money paid in by those who predicted wrongly will be used to pay him back more than he originally had. One could expect far fewer flabby, gaseous editorials if personal funds were at stake!

Some have suggested that the process of running for president has become too onerous and poisoned by moneyed interests. Local politician F.C. Morehouse thinks he has just the salve for the electoral system. Instead of allowing politicians to choose the office for which they run, Morehouse has proposed an "Office Picks the Man" system, where desirable members of the public are drafted into public service.

According to Morehouse, "The present method by which every candidate advertises his own virtues does not result in the selection of the best material." When it was pointed out to Morehouse that moneyed interests would likely have more say in who is picked to serve than leaving it to voters, he said, "Yeah, you're probably right. It appears that I am an idiot."

All this was too late, however, for poor land surveyor August Baldwin, who was kidnapped and forced to serve as city's register of deeds for four years while chained to a desk.

The day after Wilson's appearance in Milwaukee, the president stopped in Chicago for a speech. Only this time, he had an unwanted visitor. Sigmund Wisniewski was arrested on the stage where Wilson was speaking after sneaking in with the president's entourage while wearing an army uniform. When Wisniewski was arrested, police found letters in his pocket written in a foreign tongue. More embarrassing to police, however, is the fact that Sigmund Wisniewski is a rainbow trout.

On Tuesday night, after spending most of the evening teaching my neighbor's children how to roll tight cigarettes, I retired to the spare room in which the FINGER-PHONE is kept. After waiting the requisite fifty-three minutes for it to warm up, the first message it unveiled to me was from a gentleman who took vigorous umbrage to my characterization of the sinking of the Lusitania. It read:

> I have often heard the old axiom that if an infinite number of chimpanzees were given an infinite number of typewriters, one would eventually recreate the works of Shakespeare. I do say, it would take these simian scribes about four minutes to recreate your transmission of last week!
>
> You have woefully misstated the events leading up to the sinking of the U.S.S. Lusitania in May of last year. In fact, the Lusitania's sinking was the work of the British government, working in conjunction with the very European financial institutions that bankroll munitions production. With the ship's explosion, Britain will likely coax America into a war in which it has no interest, and the war profiteers will make millions of dollars to arm and equip the Alliance armies.

It was without a doubt an "inside job!"

Before the ship left the harbor in New York, Germany warned the United States that passengers sailed at their own risk, and yet there were no British vessels protecting it as it sailed into dangerous waters. When a torpedo struck the vessel, a second explosion was heard, and the entire ocean liner went down in an unheard of eighteen minutes! It is likely the first time fire has melted steel!

Even British Admiral Winston Churchill said the 1,198 passengers that perished that day were victims of "politics," not war. And American Secretary of the Navy Franklin D. Roosevelt, cousin of notorious warmonger Teddy Roosevelt, is tightly in debt with the banking illuminati who stand to finance American entry into the European conflict!

What would Germany gain by killing nearly 2,000 civilians if it baited one million American troops into entering the war? It would be a losing proposition, for sure! It is then almost certain that Churchill himself shot the Lusitania down in an effort to increase the funding and military might of the Allies. I have consulted the most knowledgeable FINGER-PHONE users, and we all agree it is a FALSE FLAG operation!

You, sir, are going to have the blood of millions of American soldiers on your hands when they enter this pointless conflict! May the fires of Hell swallow you for the damage you have wrought upon the globe!

Signed,

LUSITANIATRUTHER

P.S. – VOTE RON PAUL

What a steaming load of buncombe! Here I had just sat down to enjoy some chicken bone soup, only to find I had been magically transformed into a secret agent of the British government!

Thankfully, everyone's minds at work were not on the sinking of passenger vessels but the upcoming St. Valentine's Day holiday.

I asked dear Basil what he was getting the lucky lady in his life. He rolled his eyes and walked away. His gift must be spectacular to be such a secret.

At his station, young Philly produced two small blue pills that he claimed would be key to his Valentine's evening. He claimed one couldn't even obtain them at an apothecary, and that they – in his words – would allow him to "go all night." I told him he might want to reconsider if she lives that far away! If he has to go all night to see this young, innocent paramour, he might miss work in the morning.

With Valentine's Day soon approaching, the newspaper began running more stories regarding both romance and the absence of it. For instance, for the first time, United States residents have been blocked from receiving Valentine's Day cards from Germany. This has been terrible news for families hoping to hear from their loved ones in the Vaterland. But it has been great news to teenage boys, who now attribute their lack of Valentine's gifts to their "smoking-hot girlfriend in Germany!"

Love has also been in the news. On Wednesday, Mrs. Samuel E. Brown of Chicago filed a $17,000 lawsuit against her husband for "alienation of affections." Also named in the lawsuit was Miss Ada Cox, whom Mrs. Brown deemed a "Love Pirate" for stealing the attention of her husband. One prays the hopeless case ends up in the U.S. Supreme Court, if only so the words "Brown v. Love Pirate" are indelibly marked on the soul of our nation's judiciary!

In New York, the women's "Rainy Day Club" has disbanded, claiming its mission has been fully accomplished. The club was formed several years ago to advocate for shorter skirts to "release women from the bondage of muddy petticoats about their feet." The group, led by Mrs. Thomas A. Edison, has decided to drop dress reform as an issue because, in the words of member Mrs. A.M. Palmer, "Skirts couldn't be any shorter without - well, they just couldn't be any shorter."

In news likely to sadden Republicans, Justice Charles Evans Hughes announced that he will not be a Republican candidate for the presidency. But this week's paper also brought great news with regard to public health. According to statistics just released, only one in ten children now die in childbirth. For the first time in history, you have a better chance of surviving being born than surviving a meal at a seafood restaurant!

Word has come from Washington that the U.S. Army has developed flying vessels capable of warfare. Nearly ten years ago, inventor Alexander Graham Bell predicted that America would soon be able to wage war from the skies. In 1908, having just witnessed brothers Orville and Wilbur Wright demonstrate flying machines to the U.S. Army, Dr. Bell predicted that one day the military would have planes that flew up to 200 miles in one hour!

One can only imagine the possibilities such flight provides – consider flying from Milwaukee to New York City in the matter of mere hours! But – much like a child who discovers a stick – the first impulse is to ask, "What can I hit with this?" Clearly, using these airplanes to rain hellfire down from the skies takes precedence over mere travel expediency.

Dr. Bell said, "With a fleet composed of such battleships, marvelous things could be accomplished in a marvelously short time." And it is so true! When a flying battleship finally hovers over Germany and drops bomb after bomb, even German citizens will stop and applaud the marvelousness of America's invention before having their arms separated from their bodies.

According to another article, Milwaukee police detectives Jacob Laubenheimer and Harry Ridenour were paging through the newspaper one day when they saw the following advertisement:

> Wanted: Strong, husky young men as private detectives. Opportunity to travel all over the world. Apply at Asiatic Pacific Detective agency, Room 713, Majestic Building.

Thinking the ad was a bit too good to be true, Laubenheimer and Ridenour headed down to the agency to pose as potential enrollees. There, they met Brightley Severinghaus, who claimed to be the head of the agency.

"You look like a detective. And while it usually takes us a month to train candidates for our private force, I think I can get you through in about three weeks," Severinghaus told Laubenheimer.

"Fine," said Laubenheimer. "When do I get my first lesson?"

"You will have to put up five dollars and then the same amount every week," said Severinghaus.

Laubenheimer fumbled around and found two dollars in his pocket; Ridenour fronted him the remaining three. Laubenheimer then paid Severinghaus and, after receiving a receipt, put him under arrest.

"I thought you would make a good detective when I first saw you," said Severinghaus.

Later, a court sent him to an emergency room to have his sanity tested.

I'm sure Laubenheimer felt good about passing Severinghaus' class so quickly!

February 19, 1916

This morning I received the most peculiar transmission on my FINGER-PHONE! It appeared to be a solicitation, as it offered me the opportunity to "last longer" in order to "please my wife."

At first, I couldn't decipher what it meant. After all, I had not taken a wife, despite my advanced age of twenty-seven years. Yet, after some thought, I recognized that my mother often chastised my father for failing to wash and dry our clothes in a timely manner; after work, he was often drained, and rarely completed the task. So, I recognized how other men could use this magic salve, as nothing would please their wives more than a day's worth of clean laundry!

I enthusiastically messaged this chap back, telling him I could use all the help he could give me as my endurance was lacking. He graciously sent me a message offering to send me his most potent batch of medicine. He also asked me if he could use a photograph of me on flyers that he would be posting all over the city. I told him nothing would make me prouder!

As I walked in to work the other day, I tiptoed carefully so as not to alert the new female typist, Virginia, to my whereabouts. In order to sabotage her employment with the newspaper, I stole the "S" off of her Linotype machine, which became problematic when she had to type the headline "LOCAL MAN SHOT."

When her first print casting came up "LOCAL MAN HOT," I immediately ran it to the editor and complained that this serpent-lady had been daydreaming about a dead man! God only knows what women think of for hours on end when you put them in a man's workplace!

I was told to return to work immediately and was made to retype the story myself.

The first story on my desk was about the questionable matrimony of one Mr. Jean Harold Edward St. Cyr, who claims to be a scion of an aristocratic French family. St. Cyr has made a habit of using his position of privilege to marry wealthy widows, earning many fortunes in the process.

Yet, after a photo of St. Cyr ran in a Waco, Texas newspaper, a local resident recognized him as Jack Thompson, a former local hotel clerk and newspaper boy. In 1906, St. Cyr/Thompson married Mrs. Caroline Redfield, the widow of a Hartford, Connecticut millionaire. She was fifty-one, he was thirty-eight. She died last year – leaving her new husband millions.

Three months after Mrs. Redfield's death, St. Cyr married Mrs. William Rhinelander Stewart Smith, widow of a Wall Street speculator believed to be worth over $50 million. As a result of her new marriage, Mrs. Annie St. Cyr, as she is now known, has been ostracized from high society, and her daughter, Princess Miguel de Bragança, refuses to recognize the validity of the vows.

St. Cyr is known for his opulent parties, which one writer called "more lavish than those of Henry VIII."

Upon reading this story aloud to young Philly, he shared with me his plan to eradicate the plague of false identity throughout America. He proposed a weekly periodical that printed photographs of everyone in America, along with personal details such as job and relationship status. It would essentially be a photographic national registry where old relations could be looked up in mere minutes.

I chortled and told him such an idea would never work! Who in the world would believe their life interesting enough to share the most mundane details on a weekly basis? Plus, people are far too busy with their daily lives to update such a thing. I told him that ninety-five percent of the day, I don't want anyone to know where I am or what I am doing.

"You watch," he said. "Imagine what it will be like when it is impossible to fake your identity. When my facial registry is up and running, you will have absolute confidence that your new friends are exactly who they say they are."

He added that one day, every American would subscribe to the service, "even your parents." But he also begrudgingly conceded he primarily wanted to see how portly the girls he knew from childhood had become! (I turned down Philly's offer to invest in this hare-brained venture, as Basil told me the idea was stolen from some twin brothers Philly had once known.)

This pales in comparison, however, to the gravity of the news item featured on our newspaper's February 17th front page. "STYLES TAKE SATAN INTO PARTNERSHIP," the headline read, warning society that today's modern fashions "invite destruction of men."

At a meeting of the Fortnightly Club, Mrs. George Lewis warned that "the fashionable dress of today is an invitation to men to make improper approaches," and that now "the good woman dresses as gaudily as the evil woman." Mrs. Lewis complained about dresses that allow "full display of the nudity of the shoulder."

"On a young girl it is a shudder – on a matron, it is an awful thing," said Mrs. Lewis, adding, "May Satan fly away with it."

February 21, 1916

Given that I have discussed other FINGER-PHONE user names, perhaps you are, dear friend, wondering how I chose the very nom de guerre with which you have come to associate me.

It is quite simple. When I was a young lad, and my father was working his typical twenty-one-hour shift in the brewery, our friendly neighbor would often take me on trips over to Lake Michigan to play in the water and do some fishing. Mr. Robert A. Fetterheim was a young man of twenty-one years, with a new wife and no children – so he took it upon himself to teach me valuable lessons like how to tie knots, butcher a fish, and identify whether a body floating in the Milwaukee River is dead or alive. (The answer: You yell out, "What sound does a nut make when it sneezes? CASHEW!" And if the body does not come to life and begin laughing hysterically, it is certain all brain function has ceased.)

Unfortunately, a number of years ago, Fetterheim got very sick and had to leave his job at the factory where he helped revivify customers by putting radium in their drinking water. He quickly died and, to this day, no one has figured out what made him so sick. He lived life as clean as can be, steering clear of ol' John Barleycorn. And yet he got sick working a job that aids others in bettering their own lives – a saint indeed!

And thus, in honor of my late friend, I have taken the limited number of letters allowed and memorialized him in perpetuity. For centuries to come, let the name BOBAFETT be synonymous with kindness and compassion!

In Europe, things have taken a serious turn as fighting has begun in the French city of Verdun. Word has come down that twenty-two-year-old Donald Roper has become Milwaukee's first resident to die in the War in Europe. Roper grew up in England but relocated to Wisconsin several years ago to learn the meatpacking business. When war broke out, however, Roper heard the call of the patriot and headed to Canada to enlist for duty. It is unknown where or how he died, only that it was "somewhere in France."

Far more fortunate was British rifleman Gunner Burgoyne, who was saved from a German bullet by a Bible his mother had given him before he went off to war. The Bible, which was in the pocket of Burgoyne's jacket directly over his heart, stopped the bullet at the first chapter of St. Mark's gospel, keeping it from entering the soldier's body. One often hears that Jesus saves, but swatting away enemy artillery almost seems to be too much for even the Lord to believe!

It was also a week where violence was thwarted here at home. Would-be arsonists attempted to bomb the Nebraska state capitol building by placing a five-foot steel bomb in a furnace. The blast was subdued enough for a janitor to immediately put the fire out with little damage.

Meanwhile, police in the U.S. House of Representatives were alerted when a visitor left a long package outside the door of the congressional chamber. After several hours, the Capitol bomb squad was called to investigate. Police were relieved to find that the box only contained $4,000 in bribe money.

Citing the need to keep the United States out of the war, progressive Wisconsin Senator Robert M. La Follette announced this week that he would seek the Republican nomination for president. In doing so, La Follette will try to commandeer the progressive wing of the party in its struggle against the stalwart conservative wing.

One suggestion to keep America out of war that is bound to be less successful, however, is that of Miss May Irwin, who has written to President Wilson to urge the creation of a new federal "Department of Laughter." Miss Irwin believes that the world would be a much more peaceful place if everyone laughed a lot more; undoubtedly, her suggestion alone was meant to accomplish that goal. Perhaps one day, I will find myself typing the headline, "KAISER FOUND DEAD AT HANDS OF CASHEW JOKE."

March 4, 1916

On Tuesday, I walked into the typist room ready for work. As I approached the rear of the room, however, I noticed all my fellow employees huddled around a table, laughing.

When my friend Basil Featherstone saw me, he cleared his throat loudly, and the chortling stopped. I approached the table and saw the object of all this levity.

It was a piece of paper with the words "DOCTOR EVERBONER'S PRIAPIC RESTORATIVE" printed in large letters across the top, and below the title, there was a picture of yours truly! According to my photo's caption, I am to have said, "The only salve I trust to reinvigorate my grumpy wiener!"

"Jesus Lord! What japery is this?" I yelled.

Young Philly told me he found it taped to a street lamp pole on his way to work in the morning. He then congratulated me on my bravery in admitting my perpetual state of flaccidity, while covering his face and trying not to choke while laughing.

"I have no such problem!" I said, crumpling the paper in my hands. If I had a blood flow problem, it would not have been evidenced then, as I turned red as a radish.

It then occurred to me that this was the "please your wife"

poster I had agreed to back in January! I had been had!

Indeed, the text below my photo read:

> Is your paramour craving more? Are you having trouble
> attracting the women?
>
> In company, ladies may declare that man's skill as a lover is
> much more significant than the mere length of his
> manhood. But we all know that privately they confess to
> the contrary! In actual fact, the massive pen!s is more
> mighty and exciting! DOCTOR EVERBONER'S PRIAPIC
> RESTORATIVE will help you to become more competitive
> as a lover!
>
> If your warrior of love is too small, you may lose this war!

Of course, the purveyors of this filth knew to substitute an
exclamation point in *that word* in order to elude the decency
police. Let us hope someone will develop some sort of filter to
eliminate such ribaldry from the public square!

And with exactly whom is this "lover competition" taking place?
Obviously, if you have taken a wife, she has been untouched by
any other man. Who would wed a harlot and risk their family
name? It would seem that you are in "competition" only with
sewing and floor scrubbing!

Naturally, after his laughing subsided, Philly had a number of
questions for me. I scolded him, telling him any discussion of
one's intimate life was not a proper work topic. "That is what I
appreciate about Basil," I said. "He never burdens us with any
details of his lady conquests, which makes him a perfect
gentleman."

"I appreciate that," said Basil, rolling his eyes.

Undeterred by my admonition, Philly continued on. "How did 'pleasing a woman' become any kind of priority for anyone?" he said. "In terms of societal importance, I'd put that well behind making sure armadillos had adequate dental care."

He said he had read somewhere that men could take classes to improve their intimate "techniques" with the ladies, and he considered it all to be a rotting load of balderdash.

Philly said that for most of us, the challenge isn't giving or love of the physical variety. The real challenge is giving or receiving such love with someone else in the room. He declared that actual physical intimacy is the easy part – the hard part is finding someone that can see past your flaws enough to want to be intimate with you.

"Once you have found someone willing, or drunk enough, to form a meaningful overnight bond with you, you're really ninety-eight percent of the way there," he said.

"Teaching men love 'techniques' is about as useful as teaching a giraffe to play the harmonica," he added. "Once you have convinced a woman that you aren't harvesting cholera in your pants, the rest should be smooth sailing.

And who are these men who have trouble meeting women because their 'manhood' isn't large enough? How are women supposed to know what it's like before they even meet? It's more likely these men can't meet the opposite sex because they have food in their moustaches."

I waited patiently for Philly to finish his outrageous glandular soliloquy, which was rendered even more distasteful given that there was a woman in the room. Even though Virginia is a paper cut in human form, common courtesy demands that her delicate psyche not be subjected to the type of filth in which Young Philly was engaging.

Yet, as I looked at her across the room, she seemed to be enjoying his screed very much. It seemed she sensed my irritation with Philly and was trying to make me laugh as I stood, arms crossed, tapping my foot. She began taking pencils from her workstation and placing them in her nose, in what she likely considered to be an act of comedy.

For a brief moment, I may have succumbed to this poisonous tart's wiles and cracked a smile. But her underhanded attempt to engage in workplace camaraderie will not work on this man! It is well known that women aren't funny – the debate was settled scientifically in the 17th century when Prince Gallagher, Duke of Brittany, smashed a watermelon with a giant mallet and his wife didn't so much as crack a smile.

I guess I picked the wrong week to have to visit every lamp post in the city. Hopefully, DOCTOR EVERBONER's pills also treat the Typhoid I have likely contracted from taking down his advertisements!

The very next day, the newspaper called a meeting of employees to discuss something called "sexual harassment." Now that a woman was in the office, it appears management wanted to set out some guidelines as to proper conduct from its male employees.

The first talk was from Attorney J. Michael Brown, who set forth the strict new limits as to how uncomfortable we are allowed to make a woman in the workplace. His talk, entitled "Exposing Yourself in the Office: How Much is Too Much?" lasted about a half hour.

The next speaker, from the paper's employment department, laid out further oppressive rules, such as limits as to how many times a female employee may be asked on a date per hour. As to the most controversial rule, only three references to lady workers' bosoms per day will be tolerated. (Although Philly believes references to "dairy pillows" should be exempt, as the Wisconsin state constitution explicitly allows milk-based teasing.)

As this discussion unfolded, however, I must admit my mind was elsewhere. Over the weekend, one of the FINGER-PHONE users within the network invented the most curious service! As I noted several weeks ago, one of the challenges of the FINGER-PHONE is the permanence of its communications. Anything either posted network-wide or sent directly to a recipient lives on forever in the form of the printed page. Who knows what nefarious purposes some of these communiqués might be used for in order to one-day exact revenge!

Thus, enterprising rodent enthusiast "BEAVRLUVR" has created a service that will allay any fears one has of sending embarrassing messages. Thanks to "Blinkchat," when a message is sent to a recipient, the reader gets sixty seconds to read and process the information contained within. At the one-minute mark, a man will then break into the recipient's house, club him in the head, and seize the message. The message will then be burned, while all the furniture in the house is destroyed, the valuables looted, and the house itself is torched.

Personally, it seems the business model might need some work.

Perhaps some of the nuances of the plan might yet deserve improvement. For instance, it might be helpful to inform the recipient of a Blinkchat message that the message is, indeed, covered under the service. Otherwise, imagine the surprise they are in for!

This week also saw a breakthrough in science heretofore unknown to humanity. Surely, reader, you have heard the phrase "to have someone's number." But numerologists have literally figured out what traits can be attributable to each digit within our system!

For instance, the number one is a very masculine number, representing individuality, strength, and boldness. The number two is a distinctly feminine and receptive number, kind, peace-loving, and diplomatic. The number three is a comedic number – as any humorist knows, jokes told in threes are always the most successful.

Number four is the number for people who are afraid of zebras. Number five keeps noting that a "search party" isn't anywhere near as fun as its name would indicate. Number six always begins sentences with "I'm not racist, but..." right before he says something racist. Number seven believes the term "stool culture" is an oxymoron. Number eight always tries the "blow on hot food while it's already in his mouth" procedure, to no avail. Number nine murdered his haberdasher, dismembered the body, and mailed each limb to a girl that spurned his advances in elementary school.

Through years of research, scientists have devised a system to determine one's number through the letters in their name. It is a simple system – each letter in the person's name is assigned a number, then the numbers are added up, and the sum of the digits of that number is calculated to come up with a single number.

The number assignments are as follows:

1 - A,J,S   6 - F,O,X

2 - B,K,T   7 - G,P,Y

3 - C,L,U   8 - H,Q,Z

4 - D,M,V   9 - I,R

5 - E,N,W

Thus, the name "Frank Henry Smith" would be:

FRANK HENRY SMITH

69152 85597 14928

Adding 6 plus 9 plus 1 plus 5 plus 2 equals 23, and the numbers 2 plus 3 in the number 23 equal 5. Thus, the name "Frank" is represented by the number 5.

By the same logic, the name "Henry" is represented by the number 7 and the name "Smith" is represented by the number 6. The three names – 5 plus 6 plus 7 – equal 18 and, as before, 1 plus 8 equals 9.

In related news, everyone in America named "Frank Henry Smith" has been arrested and hanged for the crime they were most likely about to commit. Imagine all the trouble such scientific advances will one day save us!

On Tuesday, a local police officer walked by an apartment building on Third and Clarke, peered in the glass on the front door, and found William Bischoff and Helen Wollenberg engaged in what the officer termed a "soul kiss." After intently watching forty-five minutes of their activity, the officer decided he'd had enough and cited the couple for disorderly conduct, fining them five dollars for their indiscretion. Fortunately for Bischoff and Wollenberg, their libidinous activities will be long forgotten and nobody will remember their transgressions a century from now. It is not as if someone will write a book one hundred years later using their real names.

One individual sorely needing a "soul kiss" is Judge Jacob Hopkins of Chicago. Hopkins, a bachelor, recently resigned as a judge on the Court of Domestic Relations, saying that all the stories of married unhappiness had "destroyed his ideals of matrimony."

If there were only some way to follow the travails of Judge Hopkins as he looked for love! Perhaps a serial newspaper column in which a group of women tries to warm his cold, blackened heart, and each week a woman is eliminated from contention. Imagine the weekly hijinks! It could be called "All Rise for Love." Come to think of it – the American palate is far too refined for such dimwittery.

Back in the office, I finished the week telling Otto that I was currently reading A Far Country, the latest gripping novel by young British author Winston Churchill. What a literary career this young man has ahead of him! Rumor has it, Churchill is half-American; we Yankees will gladly take credit for his facility with the language.

At just that point, one of the office errand boys, Willie Britell, walked into the room and heard me extol Churchill's works. Young Willie immediately objected to my reading works of fiction.

"Fiction ain't nothin' but words made up," said Willie. "You should read things that really happened to make you smarter." He said he was currently reading John D. Billings' Hard Tack and Coffee, a stark memoir about life in the Union Army during the Civil War. It seemed unusually heavy reading for an errand boy.

"Fiction don't tell you anything about the world around you," he sneered. "Authors can just make things up. They get themselves out of logical dead ends just by creating things that could never happen."

At that point, much to our surprise, a gorilla wearing a Belgian army helmet ran into the room and ripped poor young Willie to shreds! Then, it fed his remains to a shark he brought with him, and both ran away without ever being caught. No one saw that coming!

March 18, 1916

Amid users of the FINGER-PHONE, there appears to be quite the contingent of Charlie Chaplin fans. Surely, there is much to like about the actor and his popular character, the Little Tramp, but his films have often left me cold. Most recently, all of Chaplin's films have featured increasingly sad endings, a clear sign he is seeking critical approval.

In the past, one could hold such positions without public condemnation. Yet, when I recently expressed my indifference to Chaplin's work, I was flooded with enmity from his ardent fans. I was called a "NeverTramper" who didn't understand the needs of destitute clowns. It appears, now, one is not allowed to be anything other than the most intense fan of his work; in order to show one's face in public, one must fully embrace "Chaplinsanity," as they call it.

Only recently, one was allowed to be an enthusiast of whatever moving picture they wanted, at whatever level he chose. For instance, last year, Philly went to see the popular D.W. Griffith film "Birth of a Nation" and said the viewing experience made him frightfully uncomfortable – someone was talking through the entire showing!

Yet a year later, self-described "Birthers" have now come together and formed their own fan club. In fact, their enthusiasm is so acute, they have all taken to wearing the same costume!

The change, clearly, is that lovers of moving pictures are now able to find one another via FINGER-PHONE. Whereas before there may have been several fans strewn geographically throughout the nation, now they may all communicate with one another and form armies to harass and cajole dissenters. Within their group, they create a hierarchy based on knowledge of arcane Chaplin details and harangue those who don't have the time to do such research. It would seem their time would be better spent learning how to speak to women!

On Wednesday, a woman actually approached me to chat. I was sitting at my Linotype and Virginia walked up and stood next to me, standing silently. After a healthy ten minutes, I turned to her and said, "Yes, woman?"

She asked if I had a brief moment to talk. After an obligatory full sigh and rolling of the eyes, I said I had the briefest of moments. (I have been instructed that expressing disgust at speaking to a woman is the surest way to command respect from her.)

"I am a bit embarrassed to admit this," she said while looking at the floor, "but I have answered an advertisement of a personal nature. On Friday evening, I am scheduled to accompany a man to the pictures and I have never met him before," she said. She handed me a small slip of paper she had torn from a notebook. On it was written "840 N 17th Street" in pencil.

"This is his address," she said. "I just wanted someone to have it. In case I go missing, someone will at least know where to start looking."

Why she trusted me with this information, I do not know. I told her that I promised if she were not found within one year, I would certainly consider turning over the address to the police.

She laughed. "At the very least, be ready to identify the body," she said.

"Wait!" I exclaimed. "Have you added up this gentleman's name numbers?"

"Indeed, I have," she said. "His name is Bertrand Nehls. He's a 9."

"Then I forbid it!" I yelled as I stomped my foot on the floor. "I'll be chasing your appendages down all over the city. Science is not to be reckoned with!"

She covered her mouth and giggled. She told me she was very much looking forward to meeting this young man; according to his advertisement, he is an assistant bank manager with enough steady income to purchase a home. "And he loves dogs," she added.

She said the address was merely a precaution, but that she really needed to overcome some of her recent dating failures. Just last week, she was dining with a young man when, from across the table, he began speaking to her in the "sign" language reserved for the deaf. She asked what he was doing, and he said he was secretly telling her he was having wine with a beautiful lady. She immediately walked out.

Most recently, Virginia attended a church dance for young singles. As she walked in the door, the first eligible bachelor to see her told her she was "on fire." She thought it a bit forward, but batted her eyelashes and thanked him for the compliment. "No," he said, "you're actually on fire." As she looked at her purse, she noted that some ash from her previous cigarette had fallen into the bag and smoke was now billowing upward.

"Fine," I said, sensing her excitement for her Friday engagement. "But if I actually need to use this, you'll never even know I complied with your orders."

On Friday night, I nestled into my reading chair to read my Churchill book. But concentrating was an impossible endeavor; I couldn't help but tap my foot and pull on my moustache, as I felt restless.

Then, I stood. I pulled on my jacket and hat and bolted out the front door.

Virginia was, indeed, a tarantula woman poisoning our workplace, but I could not bear the thought of her being hacked to pieces by this bloodthirsty banker. So I set out to see what exactly was happening at 840 N 17th Street.

As I approached the house, I noticed a light on in the main floor. The window was cracked only slightly, so I moved slowly toward it. I heard a man's voice telling a story he seemed to think was the funniest tale in the history of humanity, while a woman laughed at its absurdity.

I decided I should take a look around the house's garbage cans, for any sign of foul play. It seemed likely that if Virginia had lost any of her body parts, they would be found in the outdoor refuse bins.

Just then, a hound came from nowhere and lunged at me! I

tripped and fell backward, grabbing one of the metal garbage cans to catch my fall. But a racket ensued, causing the bloodthirsty assistant bank manager to rush out of his front door.

He glared at me, and barked, "Who are you?"

"Pardon me, dear sir," I said, as my innards felt as if they were being mangled by Jack Johnson himself.

"I am going door to door this evening to tell the city's residents about a unique, one-of-a-kind opportunity," I said, gulping.

"Extensive studies have shown that the number one cause of discomfort among adults between the ages of eighteen and sixty-five is having limbs that are too cold and a torso that is too warm. Perhaps you have noticed the proliferation of vests at your favorite clothier, but it is clear that vests are the exact opposite of what people desire," I said, my heart pumping acid.

"What are you talking about?" my prospective assailant uttered.

"Instead of warming our chests, what we really need is to keep our limbs warm," I said. "That is why I am proposing a new store, called 'Simply Arms,' that serves only shirt sleeves."

To demonstrate, I removed the shirt I was wearing, ripped the sleeves off, and put only the sleeves back on my arms.

"See, here I stand, bare-chested in twenty-degree weather, and I am warmer than a sack of pumpernickel loaves," I said. "A small investment on your part can ensure millions of men are able to achieve warmth with an inexpensive purchase at Simply Arms. Also, we will sell sandwiches."

He stood and stared quietly at me for what seemed like an hour. "Please leave," he said.

I walked home, vest portion of my shirt still in hand. And, I have to admit, I was still pretty cold. He was probably wise not to invest.

April 1, 1916

When I returned to the office after meeting her new beau, Virginia's was the first face I encountered.

"Seeing that your limbs are still connected, I assume your Friday night engagement went swimmingly," I said.

"It was going fine until this strange man showed up at his house," she answered.

"And what did this likely well-meaning and probably misunderstood man want?"

"It was some lunatic selling shirt sleeves."

"Oh. Well, can't blame a guy for wanting to make a living. Nobody yet knows whether a store selling sleeves and sandwiches would be profitable."

"Wait. How did you know his store would also sell sandwiches?"

I repeated her question in the way one does to buy time to think of a plausible answer.

"How did I know his store would also sell sandwiches? Turns out the guy was at my house earlier in the week. Really making the rounds, he is. Must be getting quite a few investors. Well, off to work."

I sped to my station to find my day's articles waiting for me and was shocked at the coincidence of my first task.

Today's society scandal was brought to us by a California court, which ruled that "Teddy" Slingsby, a five-year-old boy, was not actually heir to the Charles Henry Reynard Slingsby fortune. Two of Charles Henry's elder sons, Thomas and Allen, argued that their younger brother Teddy was adopted and therefore ineligible for a large inheritance. But an appeals court initially upheld Teddy's inheritance based on the child's resemblance to the father.

Several experts testified that due to the "particularly shaped ear and jaw" shared by father and son, they had to have been related. This evidently usurped evidence showing that Mrs. Dorothy Morgan Warner Slingsby had placed a newspaper advertisement the week before Teddy was born, seeking a child to adopt. And the fact that 200 witnesses testified that they couldn't remember Dorothy being pregnant or having a child.

I am personally hoping the science of resemblance is incontrovertible. I have been told on numerous occasions that I am the young John D. Rockefeller's very doppelganger. Perhaps I should begin legal proceedings immediately!

One day, maybe there will be a stage show where facial recognition scientists can tell people who their true fathers are before a paying audience. Imagine the drama such a valuable public service would provide.

Notwithstanding last week's boner, this week has brought some favorable news! I have found a new INTER-LOG user that is sure to make me the smartest fellow down at the office!

A system user, who has declared himself to be a young information wizard, has begun posting pieces that tell me "everything" I need to know about specific issues relating to current events. What a resource!

Who wouldn't want to be an instant expert on the world's affairs after reading thirty seconds' worth of the most cursory observations on a topic? Surely, when I let the boys at work know all the reasons the globe is on the precipice of a new man-created Ice Age, they will be so impressed they will carry me out on their shoulders!

Imagine the work this young man must put in! Envision all the reading of journals and books he must conduct to discern what "everything" comprises, then filtering out ninety-nine percent of that information to distill it down to just the things I "need" to know about – like why zebras make for bad accordion players. And yet, just two days ago, he posted "Everything You Need to Know about Foot Powder!"

Just this morning, this ingenious young fellow posted a delightful list entitled "Everything You Need to Know about the War in Europe." Wanting to absorb all the intricacies of European politics in less than a minute, I read it with rapt attention. I learned:

"The war in Europe was started by the assassination of Archduke Franz Ferdinand by nineteen-year-old Gavrilo Princip – a name that will be on the lips of every schoolchild for eternity!"

"French and British soldiers who are currently fighting the German aggressors are often comforted by some delicious and hearty NATIONAL BISCUIT COMPANY GRAHAM

CRACKERS, which give them the vigor to keep fighting."

"British Premier Asquith has estimated that 549,467 English soldiers have perished in the conflict so far."

"It has also been reported that N.B.C. GRAHAM CRACKERS will perish your hunger for long periods of time!"

"The United States is not yet engaged in the European conflict, but President Wilson just called for nearly 500,000 American soldiers to be prepared in case our country needs 'at any time to fight for the vindication of their character and their honor.' Wilson condemned any politicians criticizing his preparedness call as 'selfish' – as selfish as someone taking all of his N.B.C. GRAHAM CRACKERS!"

"It is rumored that the war involves somewhere between four and twenty-seven countries, but experts have said it is really impossible to know for sure."

What an indispensable list! Now I know everything there is to know about the war.

Yet, upon reading the list, one thing stood out as being mildly suspect. It seems this prodigy wouldn't even have time to attend school or hold down a job, given all the research he conducted to craft the piece. If only there were some company willing to advertise on his INTER-BLOG; perhaps he could create a model by which people could make money with their FINGER-PHONES. Let us just hope that once he does begin to accept advertising, it doesn't corrupt his message.

On Tuesday, Mrs. Viola Hood turned herself in to authorities in Salt Lake City, Utah, admitting that she engaged in an affair with a black man. Mrs. Hood said that she eloped last week with Mr. Raymond Dodds, a man whom she met while living in San Diego, California.

Dodds and Mrs. Hood were married in Salt Lake City, and, on the evening of their betrothal, the newlyweds stayed in a small rooming house where only blacks were allowed to reside. Dodds declared the room not to be fit for his beloved wife and paid for her to stay in a clean hotel where he was not welcome. The two spent the evening apart, hoping to soon depart for Chicago to begin their lives together.

When the couple turned themselves in to the police, officers asked Mrs. Hood the exact date Dodds had kidnapped her. Mrs. Hood said that they got it all wrong, that she loved him and left with him willingly. The officer nodded, and said, "Fine, but we really need to know what kind of rope he tied you up with." She once again reiterated that their love was consensual. "We get it," said the officer. "But we need to know whether the gun he threatened you with was stolen or not."

In other news of unwanted love, Miss Lillian Conklin was granted $2,500 by a judge on Tuesday for being forced to kiss wealthy mining engineer George R. Kaufman. According to Miss Conklin's account, she responded to an advertisement to be a maid at Mr. Kaufman's estate. She was alone during the interview with Mr. Kaufman, at which time he made her sit on his lap. He told her that a girl as pretty as her shouldn't be looking for housework, and kissed her once, then again, for an extended period. When his advances were rebuffed, he called the police on Miss Conklin, accusing her of being a "suspicious girl" that tried to seduce him. She then spent two nights in prison!

But after Miss Conklin's tearful testimony at trial, she was awarded the large sum of money by Magistrate Corrigan. After the decision was announced, Corrigan winked at Miss Conklin, saying, "Now you owe me one, sugar britches!"

Later that day, a speech was given by Professor M.E. Jaffa, a nutrition expert from the University of California, who declared that different sorts of food had varying effects on the moral character of human beings. Specifically, Professor Jaffa said that eating a diet of chicken helps an individual's "morality" and that chicken "brings out the finest qualities of the person's higher nature."

Beef, on the other hand, "brings out the quality of savagery," said Jaffa. "I knew an actor," he added, "who always ate large quantities of beef before playing a heavy, tragic role. He found the added savagery aided in his dramatic portrayal."

I am certainly not one to argue with a member of academia in good standing; clearly, the professor's representative sample of one of his actor friends is scientifically sound. But only if Professor Jaffa takes AWAY my steaks, he can assure himself of a savage beating! Am I right, fellows? GA!

April 15, 1916

What a valuable resource my FINGER-PHONE has become!

Some users of the device have banded together to create a remote encyclopedia that contains all the knowledge of the world! Each FINGER-PHONE owner can now deposit the contents of his skull into a network of information accessible by all users. Those users can then dial in and refine that information to make sure it is factually accurate. How could any information in this "web" be wrong if it is peer-reviewed by all of humanity?

The creation of the "INTERLOGOPEDIA" will begin to flatten the information gap between citizens who own a FINGER-PHONE. No longer will knowledge be a luxury afforded to the rich – with their expensive sets of bound encyclopedias. Marching through the snow to the library to research scientific facts will now be a relic of the distant past.

For instance, just this last week, here are some fun facts I learned through INTERLOGOPEDIA:

> – In order to keep it from attacking, read an Australian Tiger Snake a passage of poetry. They are partial to Walt Whitman.

> – Abraham Lincoln famously eschewed moustaches

because they made drinking tomato soup too difficult.

- The term "baker's dozen" originated from the Austrian practice of a baker including one extra poison pastry in a box of a dozen, prompting the kids to play a fun game in which they would guess which one it was.

- Automobiles can only run on type "O Positive" cheetah blood.

- Albert Einstein stumbled upon his Theory of Relativity after originally attempting to figure out the proper proportions for making clam chowder.

- There is only one typewriter on the continent of Africa, and it is used exclusively to type the works of Edgar Allan Poe - substituting the word "apparition" with "sandwich."

- The complete works of Shakespeare were actually secretly penned by a penguin with a very specific gift of iambic pentameter.

I was excited to impart all my newfound knowledge to my companions at work on Monday, but when I arrived, we already had a visitor. Otto's cousin Jack from nearby Tampico, Illinois was up to visit and had brought his two sons, eight-year-old Neil and five-year-old Ronnie. Otto took them on a tour of the printing presses, and the precocious little Ronnie climbed all the way to the top to see the ink being pressed on the giant rolls of paper. It appears the family had a delightful time; certainly, the Reagans are welcome back for a visit anytime.

I aimed to tell Philly all I had learned after work when we set up a time to go to the Spotted Oyster for a malty beer. First, he said we had to make a brief detour to his apartment so he could change his shirt.

His apartment was sparsely furnished, so I sat on a chair in the middle of the floor in his living room. He ducked into his bedroom, saying he would be right out. After waiting impatiently for several minutes, I opened the door to see him sitting at a desk with a small pile of white powder in front of him.

I asked him what he was doing, and in turn, he asked me if I wanted a "bump." I said I certainly would not! I am steadfastly against other people running into me, and it struck me as queer that he would suggest doing so in his own bedroom.

On the way out of the room, I noticed several dozen plastic bags of the mysterious substance piled up in Philly's closet. When we got to the Oyster, I asked him what they were, and he told me they were filled with something called "cocaine."

"It's medicine that the government just put on their prescription list last year, so I thought I'd get as much as I could before I needed a doctor's permission," he said. "I'm pretty sure the law grandfathers me in as long as I had it before the law passed."

He was no doubt correct on this point. Surely the government would not deny medicine to those who already had it in hand.

"I am delighted you have been able to keep your regenerative elixir," I told him. "In fact, I was noticing that I had never seen you more healthy and vibrant."

"I haven't slept in four days," he said.

"Amazing!" I howled, raising my beer. "Four cheers for cocaine!"

On the way to work on Thursday, I walked by a music store playing the catchiest tune I had ever heard. I popped in and asked the clerk what song he was playing, and he said it was part of the newest trend of songwriters who read the newspaper and immediately write and record a song based on that day's events! Who knows, the lyrics of that particular song may have been typed by yours truly at work. I may demand a songwriting credit when "Twelve Die in Barn Fire" becomes the best-selling record in America!

As I got to work, I settled in to type that day's first story, about the dissolution of a local educational establishment. Several months ago, the city set up its first "Hobo College," which allowed local down-and-outs to receive instruction in things like personal hygiene, vagrancy law, and public speaking. Yet it appears the college was actually a secret attempt to organize the city's transients into a "hobo union" so they would refrain from taking jobs from striking workers around the city. But yesterday, the entire operation fell apart when the college ran out of coffee and doughnuts and all the hobos walked out.

While sitting at my linotype, I noticed an eerie silence within the room. I glanced to my left, then my right, and realized one of my co-workers was missing.

"Where's Virginia?" I asked Philly.

"She took off today. Something about her father dying or something."

Typically, the newspaper's policy was that bereavement days were only given in the event three or more relatives died on the same day. So it was odd that Virginia was given a full shift off.

But even odder was what happened as I sat at my machine, typing furiously. Instead of being distracted by her presence, I was distracted by her absence. Despite the indignity of a woman working in our office, it seems her frequent jokes and companionship were something I...missed.

I kept myself busy typing up some of the day's news. The night before, nineteen-year-old James Hanlon propped a ladder up to the window of twenty-two-year-old Gertrude Crooks and attempted to enter her room. A stunned Gertrude alerted her father, Charles G. Crooks, who ran to the window with a revolver and ordered young James to leave. Hanlon scaled down the ladder, then crouched in between the Crooks' house and a neighboring home.

When Charles Crooks again ordered Hanlon to leave, the attempted burglar refused to move. So Crooks shot him in the head. The next morning, Hanlon awoke in a hospital room, not knowing he was even shot. He claimed that during the night he had been sleepwalking and had never been awake during his burglary attempt!

While at home, I decided it was only fair for me to tell Virginia of my fondness for her. To that point, I had ignored all the signs. For instance, the time I had written her name thousands of times over and over in a notebook, and the time I had drawn a cartoon dollar bill with her face and the caption "In Virginia We Trust."

Clearly, there is nothing a woman loves more than a grand pronouncement of love in a public place. This was proven during my years in high school, when I followed Agnes Mulberry behind the school to tell her that I was, in fact, deeply in love with her. She coyly responded, "You don't love me, you just think you do." What a bit of brain teasery! Then, she took off running into the woods, changed her name, and moved to North Carolina. Clearly, she was overcome by my expression of affection!

Thus began my long history of ineffective courtship. My father always counseled that it is best to leave a girl wanting more; my problem has always been leaving a girl wanting some.

Perhaps my best romance took place in college, when I met a young woman named Emma. One night, after we had first met, we were sitting on the roof of the library where she worked, and I asked her if she liked books. "I love books!" she said. I felt at that point that we had so much in common!

Yet, after that discussion, she decided to try to descend one of the Greek columns on the front of the library. Upon sliding halfway down, she lost her grip and fell to the concrete, hitting her head and losing hearing in one ear.

Bad luck for her, but what wonderful luck for me! I figured out that with her defective left ear, I had finally found a pretty young lady who would actually allow me to court her in earnest. Down at Mr. Diggler's clothing store, he often gives me a discount on pants he marks "IRREGULAR." Sometimes one leg is slightly longer or they are missing pockets or there is no fabric in the posterior region. In this instance, I had found a perfectly beautiful, if slightly irregular, woman at a discount! Courtship with a coupon!

(Sadly, young Emma kept up her practice of falling off local architectural structures until she thought she was Queen Victoria's pet cat.)

I didn't know when I would see Virginia again, so I had to plot out where I would make my confession of love. Then it came to me. Where would my amorous advances be of most use in reviving her spirits? Her father's funeral!

April 23, 1916

It is said that the great inventor Nikola Tesla has been working on a new invention that allows peoples' thoughts to be visible! His "thought camera" would look into a subject's eyes and project an image of what they are thinking onto a screen. I would certainly not volunteer for the testing of this technology, as the projection would simply be images of me eating a pickle and bacon sandwich, goats pole-vaulting, or red-headed ladies reading aloud from "Huckleberry Finn."

Tesla has also predicted some far more unlikely technologies, such as a device unconnected to any wires that a man could hold in his hand that would show pictures, play moving images, and also serve as a telephone. Good luck with that, Nikola!

It would be easy to argue that the FINGER-PHONE has now become something like Tesla's thought camera. There is now no thought that goes unpublished; there are some users of the system that dutifully report the firing of every synapse in their brain. Homeless dogs wandering the streets of the city are hoping they aren't captured by a woman with a FINGER-PHONE, as they will be made into excuses for endless histrionic self-exploration.

"AHA!" you have almost certainly said to yourself, out loud and preferably at your child's First Communion. "Are you not also engaging in such over-sharing by publishing your thoughts on your workplace goings-on and romantic interests?"

Perhaps it is true. (Although you really should pay attention to your child – as this event only happens once.) I am engaged in this INTER-WEB of information, but my life is far too important to disappear forever. What if nobody ever knew I had lived? What if a century from now, someone wanted to write a book of my life and read it on one of their handheld Tesla devices? Plus, without the FINGER-PHONE, how would I ever be able to take a hastily-designed quiz to find out which pirate disease I'd be? (I got cachexia, which is SO ME.)

I have even made a friend on this futuristic service – a young lad from Kalamazoo, Michigan that goes by the username "WillieCat." Oh, he writes the most fluid prose attacking suffragettes and prohibitionists! Progressives beware, his rib-tickling jibes are as acidic as they are insightful. There's not a dry eye in my house when he goes on a risible tirade accusing suffragettes of emasculating modern men! (In fairness, there are only two eyes in my house – it would be weird if there were more.)

Similarly, he seems to experience great joy when I try out a new catch-phrase I am attempting to coin, "PLEASE HOLD MY BEER WHILE I LEAVE YOU TEMPORARILY TO DO SOMETHING INADVISABLE." (He may have a point when he argues it should be trimmed, as brevity is the soul of wit.)

Yet, he seemed concerned about our recent discussion of my feelings toward Virginia.

"Wouldn't it be better if you told her what you thought of her in person rather than publicly?" he asked me. "What if she sees your big pronouncement coming?"

Nonsense! Nobody reads anything I write on my FINGER-PHONE! It is an insulated group of several dozen test cases strewn throughout the nation. What are the chances two people with connectivity machines would work in the same office? Infinitesimal!

During the past few days, however, I have been considering ways to strengthen my hand before telling Virginia about my feelings. Recently, judges in the city have been awarding gold medals to citizens on the street for displays of "conspicuous courage." One man, for instance, was given an award for rescuing dozens of people after a touring boat on the Milwaukee River capsized last week.

What would be better than to present my case to my beloved while adorned with a neckful of gold? Perhaps I should stand by the fruit carts downtown and wait for a hobo to finger an apple, then take him to the ground. Or, better yet, offer a hobo an apple in exchange for pretending to rob an elderly woman, at which point I would step in and save her! Certainly, the hobo union bylaws would allow such an exchange, as long as he was immediately granted two days off from hoboing.

This plan would become more feasible this week, as the local police department has decided to weaken its ranks. After studying police forces in other cities, the mayor announced that he will allow small men to become police officers. Previously, only men over five-foot-seven were allowed to pass through the uniformed ranks. Now, shorter men will be allowed to go straight to detective, as the mayor has concluded one must not be of large stature in order to solve crimes. Yet at first, these wee cops will be limited to solving mysteries of thefts under five dollars in value.

Life in America's large cities is certainly the worst it has ever been. In a speech on Monday night, E. Graham Wilson of the Y.M.C.A told of the squalor in New York City, from whence he recently returned. Graham told his audience that if Jesus himself were to visit New York, the Son of God would "openly weep."

The speaker said the fact that people are packed into buildings like "sardines" was to blame for the nation's high divorce rate. "Girls brought up in the tenement houses cannot learn to cook meals that are digestible," Graham said. "When they get married, the poor man suffers and rebels – another cause for divorce."

Before I made my pronouncement of affection to Virginia, I tried to come up with a gimmick that would guarantee her reciprocation. For instance, I have never known a lady to resist the presence of a small animal; how could she turn me away if I came bearing the gift of a pet?

At work, I had just read that a group of brothers in nearby La Crosse, Wisconsin was trying to genetically engineer a family of scentless skunks. Much like seedless oranges, these young entrepreneurs are trying to breed skunks that have no odor. In fact, skunks without their scent glands are in high demand, as they bring top dollar from pet owners. More importantly, these skunks are much more attractive to black cats who accidentally walk under a white paint roller, who normally go to great lengths to avoid skunks' romantic gestures!

Given that my affection is a steam engine that can't be slowed by any brakes known to man, I headed to Olerud's Funeral Home down on Sixth Street to tell Virginia the important news.

Wearing my only suit, I entered the front door and began eyeing the room. From the rear of the room, I saw Virginia near the front, standing near the casket and speaking softly to well-wishers.

As I began to move through the crowd, I looked to my left and saw the young man I had encountered near his house on the night of his date with Virginia! This was surely terrible news; if he spotted me, the gig would certainly be up. I resolved to dodge him at every turn so as not to be recognized.

Unfortunately, my attempts to remain undetected involved standing behind a hibiscus plant for a half hour. But when I saw a fellow mourner depart Virginia, I made my move.

With her beau out of sight, I quickly shuffled up to her near the casket.

"Sebastian?" she said. "What in the world are you doing here?"

"I had noticed you were gone from work for a couple of days," I said, realizing that I was burying the lede. "And I wanted to say how sorry I was about the loss of your father."

"Awww, thank you," she said. "I didn't think you'd pay much notice. It's not as if we're the best of friends."

I immediately saw my opening. My heart began to race as if I were locked in a cage with a wolverine. In trying to remember the speech I had memorized to declare my affection, two opposite emotions crashed into one another – those of concentration and relaxation. At that moment, I'm not sure if I could have named the president of the United States if asked.

"Actually, that's something I came here to talk to you about," I said.

Just then, I felt a tap on my shoulder.

"I see you're wearing sleeves today," said the voice behind me. It was her dreaded, handsome paramour who I had confronted late that night outside his house.

"Ha, yes. I assumed today's occasion meant I should come fully armed," I mumbled, as I began to sweat through my suit jacket.

"Wait – you two know each other?" Virginia asked.

"No, no, no," I said. "I think maybe we crossed paths on a business opportunity some time ago."

As he lifted his finger to clarify, I cut him short.

"What's really important is that we are here to pay tribute to your father, who was a great man," I said. "I can't imagine things being the same without him."

"That is very kind," she said. "Did you know him?"

"Oh yes," I said, knowing that the man in the casket could not disprove my thesis. "Such a generous man. Titan of the community. So giving."

My rival immediately became a stowaway on my train of praise. "I agree completely," he said. "I often golfed with Herman, and I knew him to be the most decent human I had the fortune of knowing. His charitable work was unmatched."

"Really?" Virginia asked. "Given his work as a city tax collector, I can't imagine too many people thinking he was all that charitable. You really knew him well, Bertrand?"

His name was Bertrand! Surely the mark of a scoundrel!

"Of course," he said, looking around to see if anyone nearby would expose his obvious ruse. "In fact, I always hear people down at the Madison Club saying they thought he might have been the greatest human who has ever walked the earth. Had he lived, clearly the papacy was not out of reach."

I felt I was being bested by this fool in the sympathy Olympics.

"I am finding it difficult to go on with my life, given that a man of his stature is no longer with us," I said. "The world will likely be an arid, desolate husk of what it once was given that this transcendent man gave his life for its citizens."

"He choked on some pickled herring," said Virginia.

I knew it was time to pour it on, so as not to be outshone by the chisel-faced baboon competing for her affection.

"I only wish to once more give him a hug as a show of gratitude for humanity," I said, walking toward the casket. I leaned over and wrapped both arms around the corpse, knowing that the cowardly Bertrand would not rise to the occasion in such a manner.

Yet the stand holding the casket appeared to not be of the most robust construction. As I embraced the old buzzard, I felt the casket give way and fall to the floor. While attendees screamed in horror, I realized that, upon hitting the ground, Virginia's father had exited the casket and rolled about five feet on the floor.

When describing the look of someone who has experienced a horrific event, one could employ the metaphor that it was "as if they had seen their dead father fall from a casket and end up at their feet." Yet this is exactly what happened, and it reflected on Virginia's face.

"You should probably leave," she said.

I didn't even get the chance to give her the scentless skunk.

May 1, 1916

My failed attempts at wooing Miss Virginia would normally occupy all my waking thoughts, but there is no time! Skullduggery is afoot!

According to the news department, it has been discovered that German spies have attempted to influence American elections in order to install politicians more favorable to the cause of the Hun!

According to documents seized from German operatives, United States Senate candidate Oscar B. Colquitt of Texas has made a secret deal with German-American groups, in which he has pledged support for the Kaiser. In exchange, he expects to earn all the German-American votes in the state, which exceeds the size of Germany itself by 50,000 square miles!

It is further believed that a central headquarters for controlling American elections by German spies has been established in New York City. This office is run by Bernard H. Ridder, editor of the New York Staats Zeitung, who is to recruit candidates with secret German sympathies in order to keep America out of the war in Europe.

Surely any elected officials found conspiring with a nation that may soon become our adversary will be tried for treason! Thankfully, this was merely a U.S. Senate seat; such subterfuge is unthinkable at the presidential level.

On my walk to work on Monday, I dreaded my impending interaction with Virginia. Clearly, I will have to put off any declarations of affection until she forgets the sight of her dead father rolling around on the floor of the funeral home. I suspect I will need to give it at least two or three days for her to purge it from her memory completely.

As I walked down Third Street, I noticed a small booth on the right-hand side of the road that hadn't been there on Friday. Upon further inspection, it was one of the new "shaveaterias" that have been popping up all over town. These are small structures in which a man can go to get a shave without having to go to a barber shop.

As I inspected this particular shaveateria, I noticed it was stocked with soap, brushes, razors, towels, coconut butter, witch hazel, bay rum, face lotion, talcum powder, and a wash bowl. A rumor around town is that these booths are expected to take their place next to the new "waiterless" restaurants, where everyone helps himself to food. What other wonders will this modern sharing economy produce?

When I got to the typist room, I immediately ducked behind a bookcase to survey the lady situation. Seeing none, I darted to my Linotype machine and began banging out the first handwritten story on my workstation. Appropriately enough, it was about Kansas City man Eddy Foley, a jilted lover who found that he was not invited to his former girlfriend's wedding to another man. To get revenge on this woman, for whom he clearly still had affection, Foley put on his best suit, showed up outside the wedding, and began picketing the event "in approved labor union style."

The story, of course, ended with the least surprising words in the English language: "He also said he had been drinking."

In the oddest news of the week, after a nine-year-old Chicago boy was severely burned, nineteen local fraternity brothers donated a square inch of skin to the young lad. Amazingly, the operation proved a success and the boy healed with the help of, as the newspaper story put it, "a crazy quilt of cuticle."

After I finished typing a story about Republican Charles Evans Hughes' declaration that he will never accept the party's nomination for president, I felt a warmth on the side of my face. As I slowly turned left, I realized it was the intense glare of one Virginia Hansen, fellow employee at the Milwaukee Post.

"Shame that Hughes is dropping out," I said, hoping to talk about literally anything other than my accidental desecration of her father's corpse.

After a calculated pause, she answered, "You like Hughes, huh?"

Yes! I had successfully changed the subject to something completely uncontroversial – politics.

"For all I care, all the Republicans can take a walk," she said, "until they demonstrate their commitment to letting women vote."

Oh no! What had I done? I immediately wished I could change the subject back to something less contentious, like the time I slid her dead father's body across the floor like a shuffleboard disk.

"You think Woodrow Wilson is better for women?" I asked. "He doesn't support the women's suffrage amendment either."

"Oh, he'll come around," she said. "He's just playing coy to get elected. And he's kept us out of the war in Europe and supports banning alcohol, so he's got my vote."

Perhaps this was a revenge plot on her part - I could feel my temperature rising, while a bead of sweat hung from my moustache.

She is one of THEM.

"That reminds me," she said, "I need to ask off from work on Monday, May 15th so I can march in the big suffrage parade. Thousands of principled women will be there and I can't miss it."

Or at least, I thought that is what she said. Using only my eyes, I begged Basil to come splash some water on my face so I didn't lose consciousness. He flashed me a quick, wry smile and went back to setting type for the afternoon edition.

Ever since it was announced, the upcoming Women's Parade has been mired in controversy. For beginners, two competing groups have been trying to recruit women to their side, each advocating different tactics and principles. Mrs. Alice Paul of the Congressional Union recently announced that, while a new women's political party will be forming, there will be no woman running for president in 1916. Conversely, Anna Howard Shaw of the competing National American Woman Suffrage Association, or NAWSA, says forming a political party is a bad idea, as it will alienate members of both parties with whom the women's groups need to work hand-in-hand.

The animus between the groups has spilled over into parade preparations as well. For the upcoming parade, the National American Woman Suffrage Association has manufactured thousands of straw hats with yellow ribbons that will cost them fifteen cents, but Congressional Union members will be wearing five-dollar hats that they call the "women's party hat." This expensive headwear, billed as a "creation of silk, straw, and braid adorned with rosettes of purple, gold, and white," has been derided by the NAWSA as hats meant only for rich women.

But perhaps the most forceful blow was struck this week by the NAWSA, when they introduced a new suffragist parrot that will be marching with them in the parade. The colorful bird, unoriginally named Votes, says such things as, "Votes for women" and, "Polly's going to march."

Surely, Votes the parrot has been well-trained. (To me, the fact that there are ANIMALS WHO CAN TALK should be front-page news every day of the year!) Yet parade organizers aren't quite sure what type of home Votes lived in during his early years; as he occasionally blurts out the phrase, "Bitch, make me a sandwich."

And yet, Votes the parrot is still likely more popular with women than I am. There was actually a time when I thought I could provide guidance to others that had trouble meeting members of the opposite sex.

Take my college roommate Boomer Mills, who often had trouble talking to females. Women were new to campus, and there was one young beauty we frequently noticed; she always wore a fashionable dark green coat, so we granted her the sobriquet "Evergreen." I made a wager with him that I could get

Evergreen to our dorm room. He announced loudly that, if I did, he would buy me "a bottle of the finest whiskey," before mumbling under his breath the important addendum, "I can afford."

One day, I spotted my comely target and moved in. I nervously explained the whole plot to Evergreen and told her if she were to come to our room for just one drink, I would split the bottle of fine whiskey with her. Her eyes widened, and she exclaimed, "I am so in."

The date having been set, I snuck Evergreen into our room, dressing her as a haggard milk deliveryman to sneak her past the dormitory security guard. Once inside, Boomer presented us with our winnings; although our spoils appeared to be a bottle of Old Crippled Buzzard whiskey, the foulest of spirits! Rumor has it, when not being ingested, it is often used to degrease motorcycle tires at the nearby Harley-Davidson plant.

Upon taking the first swig of the poison, I emptied the contents of my stomach directly on Evergreen's immaculate coat. She tore out of the room, never to be seen again. She didn't even abscond with her share of the booty on the way out. What a boner I was!

It was no surprise, then, that I had made a dog's dinner of my situation with Virginia. It is widely known that when pursuing a young lady, dumping her dead father on the floor of the funeral home is frowned upon. It is one of the ironclad rules of love, right behind "never try to steal the girlfriend of a man with a beard." (If a woman is willing to put up with a man growing a face sweater, her love is unconditional.)

I tried to remain upbeat, despite the knowledge that Virginia was likely spending her nights in the embrace of that filthy troglodyte Bertrand. No doubt they are at his home at this very moment enjoying a selection of exotic rums while she gazes at his diamond-cutting chin.

Yet even if this were the scenario, all would not be lost. I have long thought it much more advisable to pursue ladies who have already taken a lover. If one is fishing for companionship in the sea of women, one's lure must be better than all others in the ocean. Yet, if you focus your attention on a woman with a beau, all you have to do is be better than that one fellow. Why compete with the world when you can simply demonstrate your superiority over one fallible sap?

But how? What could I do to best this festering cavity known as Bertrand?

This was the topic of last Thursday night, as I found myself elbow-deep in a lager at the Spotted Oyster with Philly. I had not yet explained the inter-office tension between Virginia and myself, and he seemed delighted to learn the news.

"Wait. I thought you hated her?" he said.

"Well, it's a love-hate situation," I said. "Or hate-love now, depending on the perspective."

He asked how I planned on erasing the execrable Bertrand from my future autobiography.

"Perhaps I can borrow some of your magical cocaine?" I asked. "It seems to turn men into super-people, capable of conquering any task."

"No, I think that would be inadvisable," he said. "Cocaine

simply takes people who are already superior and makes them even more superior. You need some work on your baseline superiority."

"How about you write a book of fiction that describes your ideal romance, then hint to her that she is the main character?" he said.

"Write an entire book specifically to tell someone in secret how in love you are with them?" I asked. "That sounds like the greatest waste of time possible! I might as well stand outside her house holding a Victrola over my head as it plays a romantic tune."

"You'd be surprised," he said. "That's basically all fiction is – young men cloaking their desire for a woman in flowery prose. Or dirty old men writing about young women and pretending it's not gross because it's 'fiction,'" he said. "In a work of fiction, you can confess unpopular opinions with plausible deniability by saying it's merely what the characters think."

"It would take me years to write a book," I said. "I can barely read one in under two months." I looked down, defeated.

"Alright, try this. Find a shared interest and demonstrate to her a feat of excellence within that subject," Philly said.

"Go on."

"For instance, if she enjoys the work of Emily Dickinson," he said, "memorize a Dickinson poem or two and casually quote a line in the office here or there. That way she won't think you committed them to memory simply to impress her."

"Dickinson seems to be a morose subject on which to base

everlasting love," I said. "I'm just supposed to approach her and say, 'I measure every grief I meet with narrow, probing eyes. Also, may I kiss you on the mouth?'"

"Well, make it something else, then. Perhaps you share an affinity for certain political causes. Show her that you have committed yourself to an issue with which she agrees," he said.

My mind skipped back to the terse discussion of politics in the office two days ago. "Most certainly not!" I ejaculated.

"Do you want to deflower her or what?" Philly asked.

"I am not certain what you mean, but—wait a minute!" I yelled.

It all occurred to me in a bright flash. "What if I were to walk side-by-side with Virginia in the upcoming suffragette march?" I asked.

Philly spit his beer out. He paused, then began laughing uproariously.

"It's insane, but it might just work!" he yelled in between guffaws. "I would pay a month's salary to see you in the middle of a crowd declaring solidarity with a gaggle of suffragettes!"

"What man would ever want a woman like those ladies?" I said. "Isn't that why they all travel in packs together? Because no decent fellow will have them?"

"Oh, they're not so terrible," said Philly. "I am actually rather fond of ladies who prefer the company of other ladies."

"I'm not sure I quite know what you're getting at," I said.

Philly shrugged, held his palms skyward, and curled the corners of his mouth down.

"You know, women who are sort of like men," he said.

I began spitting my beer back into the glass, forming a pillow of froth on my moustache.

"Like, a tomboy?" I said. "Like Jo March in Little Women? Don't young ladies grow out of such behavior when they finish their schooling at grade five?"

"No," he said. "Ladies who prefer the company of other ladies."

"I'm still not quite sure what you mean," I said, scratching the crown of my head.

"Women who are...involved with others of the fairer sex."

"Well aren't they all in each other's business all the time? I should say the ladies at church are very much involved in the affairs of their friends. They gossip incessantly!"

He took a deep breath, appearing to be well down the path of losing patience with me.

"Ladies who prefer other ladies romantically," he said. "Ones that lay down with their own kind."

I shot to my feet.

"You have just mentioned the love which must remain unnamed!" I thundered, pointing at him.

I had read about such types of women, but only in the forbidden Sapphic tales of Ancient Greece. As these "women" didn't procreate, there could not be any of them left in these modern days!

"Would you please just sit and keep your voice down?" he said. "It's no big deal. I just find them attractive."

I whipped my head left and right, thinking this was some sort of prank. Were our office mates crouching behind the bar waiting to admit to the japery? Suddenly, a number of conflicting thoughts began wrestling for supremacy in my brain.

"So...if you like women who don't like men, that seems to be a pretty sub-optimal plan for finding romance," I said. "And if it is men who normally prefer women, and you are fond of women who prefer women, does that mean..."

I stopped and gasped.

"You prefer men? Like in Moby Dick?" (I had read a criticism of the book which accused Melville of making the whale a homosexual.)

"Are you going to ask me to marry you?" I inquired, chugging the remainder of my beer.

"No, ass," he said. "I definitely like women."

"And yes," he continued, "it makes no sense that I would find attraction in those who could never be attracted to me. But maybe that is what it is. Maybe the absence of pressure to be romantic is in itself romantic. Lord knows it's hard to be yourself around a lady when she sees you as her best chance for marriage and children. Maybe I'm like a lady who has a special affinity for priests."

He paused. "Find yourself a pretty woman whom you can talk to about baseball and combustion engine maintenance - and yes, even other women - and you've struck gold, my friend."

It surprised me that his argument failed to horrify me.

"Imagine two women living together!" I said, still puzzled. "Who would do the chores and cook the food? And how would each of them know to stop talking so the other one could get a word in? Where would I even find one of these mythical lady-lovers? Down at the Forbidden Love Emporium and Delicatessen?"

"You're a fine young man," I told him. "You should find a lady who can reciprocate your love. Perhaps ask Basil for some tips. He probably has feminine piping birds surrounding him at all times!"

"You really are clueless," he said.

"There's a ladies golf tournament in town next weekend," I told him. "You should go. What better place to find a wife?"

May 16, 1916

During one of our lengthy FINGER-PHONE discussions last week, I told my good chum WillieCat that I would be attending yesterday's suffragette parade. He responded that he thought it would be a tactical mistake on the level of General George Custer's sojourn to Little Big Horn. Yet WillieCat seemed to delight when I told General Custer he should "PLEASE HOLD MY BEER WHILE I LEAVE TEMPORARILY TO DO SOMETHING INADVISABLE." My signature phrase never fails!

I rose early in the morning, as I wanted to take extra care to look good for Virginia. If she saw me looking my best and supporting the right of women to vote at the march, there surely would be no way she could resist me! Let's just say I may have put a little extra wax in my moustache, if you know what I mean.

I also needed to get to the office and get some work done early in the morning, so it would be less noticeable when I left around lunch time for the parade. Normally, under newspaper rules, we were granted three minutes for lunch. I was hoping that if I got nearly all my work done, I could stretch it to maybe ten.

The news was primarily about the presidential race anyway and, with more than five months to go until the election, who was even paying attention to politics? It's clear that Teddy Roosevelt is going to win in any event – bookmakers are already offering two-to-one odds that TR will be the next president.

Yet evidently, Supreme Court Justice Charles Evans Hughes has suggested he would be willing to run against Woodrow Wilson as a Republican under the following conditions:

1. Nobody would run as a Progressive candidate against him – thereby sucking away Republican votes and handing the election to Wilson, as happened four years ago.

2. Nobody with a name that rhymes with "Freddy Hose-a-Belt" also runs.

3. In the event he wins, Thursdays are pants-optional.

4. He can pick one foreign leader to call "fat," because it would be "modern-day presidential."

As lunchtime loomed, I was wondering if I had made the right decision to pretend that I supported the crazy notion of women voting. What if Virginia actually believed that I had converted to her beloved progressivism? If we were to become lovers, what ideological prison would I then live in for all eternity?

While ruminating upon relationship jail, I was reminded of the recent case of James Mansfield, who was arrested for narcotics possession based on information provided to the police by his fed-up girlfriend, Marie Miller. During the trial, Miss Miller said she had turned him in for his own good and had obtained a position for him at a reputable business if the government dropped the charges.

In a surprising move, the prosecuting attorney told the couple that he would drop the charges if they were to get married! Mansfield immediately said no, claiming he didn't believe in hasty marriages and had no money. Miss Miller immediately jumped in a taxi, obtained a marriage certificate from the county, brought it back and forced Mansfield to marry her on the spot. What a happy marriage it will be now that Miss Miller knows her husband preferred actual prison to living with her!

As eleven o'clock struck, I slipped out the back door and headed for Fourth Street, where the parade was to begin. I didn't really know at all what to expect; in other cities, these "women's demonstrations" had turned into rowdy affairs. Last week in New York City, the police were called when Bolton Hall, Emma Goldman, Jessie Ashley, and Ida Raub Eastman gathered to give speeches about something called "birth control," which they claimed would bring "a better, purer race."

They handed out pamphlets entitled "Why, and How, the Poor Should Not Have Many Children" before the police broke up the event. (But the joke is on them! If the poor refuse to have children, who would work the printing presses to make their beloved pamphlets!)

As I made my way toward the front of the parade, I began seeing the straw hats with yellow ribbons everywhere. As I turned the corner onto Fourth Street, it resembled a field of dandelions with thousands of yellow, bobbing hats.

As I twisted my way through the crowd of suffragists, I kept an eye out for these mythical lady-lovers Philly had warned me would be in attendance. If they were there, they hid their predilections well; all these ladies seemed perfectly respectable.

Perhaps they have secret meetings to learn how to go undetected – or maybe Philly simply has an overly vivid imagination!

I dreaded being recognized, so I ducked into an alleyway to apply my disguise. Over my moustache, I applied a slightly larger false moustache, secured with a piece of string around the back of my head. (Thinking ahead, I had colored the string black to match my hair, so it was completely undetectable!)

The plan was thus – if I saw Virginia, I would immediately remove the disguise and approach her. If she saw me first, she clearly wouldn't recognize me, which would give me the chance to quickly ditch the false moustache and approach her as myself a few minutes later.

Near the rear of the parade, a short, portly young woman called out to me. I approached her and saw she had some large pieces of paper attached to sticks, presumably to make signs.

"Are you marching with us today?" she asked.

"There is no more important thing in the world to me than to shred the stable social and economic framework that men have created over thousands of years. So, yes," I said, trying not to break character.

"Okay, ummm... I'm not sure that's really our message, but we're happy to have you," she said. "You can use these tools to make your own sign."

"Thank you, fellow woman enthusiast," I said, grabbing a sign and a paintbrush. I quickly scrawled my message out, grabbed a straw hat from the booth and lined up, jumping up and down in order to see if I could glimpse my beloved Virginia among the thousands of marchers.

I worked my way as close to the front of the parade line as possible, knowing Virginia would want to be in a prominent place in the queue. I was several inches taller than the thousands of women that surrounded me, so I was able to survey the crowd fairly easily. I held my sign down by my feet, as I suspected it would block my view.

At that point, I heard a male voice yell "Sebastian!" I quickly wheeled around to face the sidewalk, where a counter-demonstration was taking place, and there I saw my old college chum, Boomer Mills!

Boomer had gathered with a group of anti-suffragists and was holding a sign that said "DO NOT OVER-STARCH MY PANTS."

"How did you know it was me, old pal?" I asked. "I'm in disguise," I said, pointing to my slightly more robust moustache.

"Uh, it must have been your earlobes that gave you away," he said, laughing. "What in hellfire are you doing cavorting in this pit of vipers?" he asked.

"I'm deep under-cover," I whispered. "And I would die if you told anyone you saw me here."

"OH YEAH?" he bellowed. "Then you need to do me a favor!"

"Anything," I said.

"You're still working at that newspaper, right?" he asked.

"I am."

"As it happens, I am just starting a new business venture, and I could use a little publicity," he said.

Boomer was always famous for his shady ventures. He was perhaps most famous for the time in college he actually poured tap water into used bottles, told people it was free of contaminants, and they actually purchased them! At one point, seeing restaurants moving to a "farm to table" ethos, Boomer tried to start his own "stream to mouth" restaurant where diners could pluck a salmon out of the water with their teeth like a bear.

"But," I told him, "I don't write the articles. I just type them for the people that do."

"Hey, Simon," he said, turning to one of his buddies, "have you met my feminist friend-"

"Okay, okay!" I said, cutting him off before he could blow the lid off my scheme. "Send me what you want in the paper, and I'll try to slip it in."

"You're a good pal," he said. "You better get back to your sewing club. The parade is starting."

I glared at him.

"Solidarity, sister," he sneered as I walked away.

The parade had begun down Fourth Street, so I quickly assimilated back into the crowd. As we marched, I tried to go about twice as fast as the suffragists around me, snaking my way through with my shoulders turned perpendicular to the churning mass. As I passed through, a few of the marching ladies even patted me on the shoulder to tell me they appreciated my attendance, as their husbands refused to participate.

In fact, I got so wrapped up in the approbation I was receiving, I had forgotten to wave my sign up high! If they were pleased with me for merely being there, think of the praise I would receive when they saw I was a true believer in their brand of lady politics!

Yet, when I proudly raised my sign, I began to hear nothing but gasps and murmurs.

"What is that supposed to mean?" asked an elderly woman of about thirty-five.

"It means what it says," I answered, reading the text of the sign aloud. "THUMBS UP TO TWO-LADY LOVING."

"What is wrong with you?" yelled a young, brunette woman on my left.

"Do you think we're all lesbians?" one woman yelled at me.

"I'm not sure what that means, but I'm trying to tell you I'm on your side!" I said. "The more women lay with each other, the better!"

Suddenly, the yelling around me got much louder, and I began to suspect my declaration of solidarity was not having its intended effect.

"Are you some sort of deranged fetishist?" one woman yelled.

I had to scream to make myself heard at this point.

"NO!" I yelled. "You're getting me all wrong. I love lesbians!

I LOVE LESBIANS!"

Just then, I looked to my right and saw the face of my beloved Virginia, eyes fixed on me and mouth open so far one could have inserted a typewriter with ease.

"Seb-Sebastian?" I heard her say. Fortunately, I was still in disguise!

"No, it's not me. It's some other guy!" I yelled, before dropping my sign and making a run for it. On my sprint back to the office, I was buoyed only by the fact that my disguise had not fallen off - keeping my anonymity intact.

My legs churned like steam pistons until I finally got back to the rear door of the Milwaukee Post. Thankfully, it appeared my absence went unnoticed.

As I settled back into the chair facing my Linotype, sweat cascading down my forehead, Basil Featherstone walked up behind me and urgently handed me an article that had clearly just been finished.

"This one's a rush job," Basil said.

I looked down at the headline: "LOCAL PERVERT RUINS WOMEN'S MARCH"

June 7, 1916

Perhaps, friend, you noticed I have been gone for longer than usual. With every lady in the city looking for someone of my description, I thought it best to remain incognito for several weeks. Fortunately, my thoughts on the FINGER-PHONE are virtually unread – although my pal WillieCat couldn't stop gloating after having warned me not to attend the parade. Even more fortunately, the city police put officers under five-foot-seven on the case to find me. Clearly, they didn't consider my capture a priority.

But I also haven't been able to write as I have had the most incredible week!

Late last month, Milwaukee Post political reporter Dirk Calloway told me he was making the journey south to the Republican National Convention – to be held in Chicago this week. When I told him that sounded like a singularly stupendous adventure, he let slip that he was allowed to take one other Post employee to help him with the administrative tasks of covering so many events.

"I'll do it!" I yelled, before he even offered. I figured I could use some time out of town – away from Virginia and the leering eyes of law enforcement. Plus, the Republicans were about to pick the man that would most surely become the next president of the United States. Who could resist being in a place where the seeds of the next century of history would likely be planted?

With Chicago being over seventy miles away from Milwaukee, the train ride took nearly a full day – during which time, Dirk told me he had originally planned to ask Virginia to accompany him. Fortunately, he dodged that bullet, seeing as how she couldn't possibly provide the quality of company I can.

While we rode the train south on Friday morning, he asked about the wooden box in my possession that contained my FINGER-PHONE. I couldn't reveal to him my secret, so I simply told him it was a typewriter I brought on trips.

"You're not going to be doing any writing," he said. "That's reserved for the professionals."

"I assure you I can write," I told him.

"Imagine if just anyone could say whatever they wanted and the whole world could read it," he said, lighting a cigarette. "It would be unbridled chaos, with people making unfounded claims and casting baseless aspersions. No, my friend, it should be left to the professionals. In fact, centuries ago in Ireland, writers had to study for ten years to have a literary career. Then, they had to pass ten written exams to write for the public. I'd be more in favor of a system like that than one where everyone can just blurt out whatever ill-considered, capricious thought inhabited their head at any given time."

"I think I could surprise you," I said. "After all, I spend all day reading and typing."

"You read and type other people's words," he said. "That's like saying I can write concertos like Mozart because I can play the harpsichord."

I suspect he could tell I was getting irritated, as I began chewing on the corner of my moustache - a nervous habit I have had since I grew my first facial hair at age fourteen.

"Alright, let's see," he said. "Do you have any writing samples?"

At this point, I found myself in quite a pickle. I clearly did have writing samples, but they were in the form of FINGER-PHONE observations! If I were to tell him about this new technology, and my role in advancing it, he surely would report me to my superiors at the newspaper, who would then permanently ban me from the office!

"I guess I do not," I said.

"We shall speak of it no more," he huffed, opening a copy of The Chicago Tribune newspaper and folding it to display a story in that morning's edition. He handed it to me, showing me a headline that screamed, "HOW TO WIN YOURSELF A NEWSMAN."

Given the high esteem in which newspaper reporters are held, they are clearly quite in demand - especially during events in which tens of thousands of convention-goers would be pouring into town. So, the Chicago daily newspaper wanted to give the ladies from out of town some tips on how to make themselves more attractive to local reporters, that they may win the lottery of love and score one of society's most admired professionals.

"The Newspaper Man - of a class as keen as these times have developed - often grasps the character of a woman through the clothes she wears," read the article, as it proceeded to offer perfume and hairstyle tips. Yet the provenance of the story became suspect when it suggested women become "intimate with the details of paleontology" and "learn to love men with a claw for a left hand." One can only presume the reporter penning the article shared these traits.

"You see," Dirk said, "men of the press are in high demand from members of the opposite sex. So I hope to see as little as possible of you, as I will most likely be selecting a lover from a select group of competing women."

"Fine by me," I said, knowing I would need some free time to write the missive I am currently composing.

On Saturday morning, I walked out of my hotel on Van Buren Street and headed one block west to Michigan Avenue, where the preparedness parade was to take place. The streets were teeming with flag-waving patriots showing their support for a buildup of American armed forces should we become involved in the horrific conflict burning Europe to the ground.

For as far as the eye could see, every road was lined ten-deep with parade-goers. My only job was to talk to them and write down what they said, which would have been much easier if I wasn't averse to speaking to humans in person. (Which is why I am typing this to you now!)

At one point, I stopped and talked to a boy in his early teens who said he had been looking forward to the parade ever since it was announced.

"What's your name, boy?" I asked.

"Edward Pence, sir," he said. "I live just a few blocks away over on Lowe Avenue."

I told him he was young to be so involved in politics.

"I'm not young, I'm fourteen," he boasted. "And one day, I'm going to have a grandson that grows up to be the Vice President of the United States."

Quite a boast indeed! And oddly specific!

Along the parade route, every window was filled with faces. Some people had climbed streetlight poles, and others balanced perilously on chairs and tables to get a look at the marchers. I asked a local police officer how large he expected the crowd to be and he said, "A million, easy."

The marchers came in waves, hour after hour. There were the War of '61 veterans, singing patriotic songs. There were 3,000 pretty phone operator girls all marching in line, as men loudly yelled compliments their way. (How flattered they must have been!) Some business owners decided to march with their own employees, and even the German Club of Chicago had several hundred marchers in the parade.

As the bands marched through the parade route, chants picked up among the masses lining the streets.

"Prepare!"

"Providence is surely in favor of preparedness!"

"It seems it would be in the United States' best interest to be ready in the event we need to go save the world from potential ruin at the hands of the Central Powers, and yes, we realize this is a really long chant, but we thought it was important to be perfectly clear about the goals which we aim to achieve!"

Not everyone was ebullient about the parade, however. Strewn across a building on Michigan Avenue was a large white cloth sign that read:

TO THE MARCHERS: There are 100,000 of you. You are not the ONLY patriots. Two million farmers, half a million mine workers, and organized labor throughout AMERICA are AGAINST what you are marching for. Are you SURE you are right?

Needless to say, this act of insurrection did not cause parade-goers to reflect on the nature of war and man's role in armed conflict. After the sign caught the eye of a captain of the South Park police, officers ran up to the third floor of the building and tore it down, arresting the men who created it. Mrs. W.I. Thomas, a professor at the University of Chicago and member of the Women's Peace Party, had let the sign-makers into the organization's office (one of them was her son) and allowed them to post the treasonous banner. In order to maintain journalistic balance, I remarked in my notes that the men should only be given twenty years in prison and not the more extreme death-by-firing-squad.

After the parade, I met up to trade notes with Dirk at Charley Hansen's saloon on Irving Park Boulevard. Oddly, there were few people in the establishment. I asked the barkeep, who introduced himself as the owner, where all the people were. He said the bar had only recently re-opened after financial difficulties.

Hansen's story went thusly: Evidently, a wealthy customer

named Mads Jacobsen had left two hundred dollars in his will to spend on a party in his own honor at Hansen's saloon. After Jacobsen's recent funeral, two hundred mourners descended on Hansen's tavern and drank, as provided in the will, two hundred dollars' worth of "beer and whiskey and wine and whatever."

When the last of the besotted revelers stumbled out, Charley Hansen asked for payment. Yet only then did Jacobsen's attorney read the fine print of the contract: The party was supposed to be paid for out of the $2,000 Jacobsen had left his wife from his policeman's pension. But Mrs. Jensen had passed away two years previously, and Mr. Jensen had never replaced her with another beneficiary. Thus, the money was never paid out and poor Charley Hansen had to eat the cost.

I whispered to Dirk that we should pay the fine man an extra gratuity when we finished our whiskeys, just to help the old man get back on his feet.

"Absolutely," Dirk said, as he downed the remainder of amber sustenance from his glass.

Just then, Dirk's head snapped around.

"Do you hear a telephone ringing?" he said.

"I most certainly do not," I answered, cupping my hand to my ear to get a better listen.

"I had better go check to see," he said, getting up from the bar and briskly walking outside. He did not return.

"Looks like your buddy stiffed you," Hansen said.

"Yeah, you should get ready to host his funeral here tomorrow," I joked, throwing down a dollar and walking out the door.

After drunkenly stumbling into my hotel room, I plugged my FINGER-PHONE in to see if anyone was awake to talk. Visions of what Virginia might be up to at that moment swelled in my brain, and I began scribbling her name over and over on a piece of paper.

I sent a message to WillieCat, but he failed to answer promptly. I was worried – rarely is he unable to converse, even at a late hour. What if some tragedy befell him? What if he had met a lady and no longer needed my companionship?

I began to browse other INTER-LOGS to see what I had missed during the day. There was much discussion about user "CarlisleJay," who had been banned from using his machine for frequently spreading unfounded malicious rumors about public figures. CarlisleJay is perhaps most famous for claiming that Woodrow Wilson is an alligator, frequently pointing out that nobody yet had proven him wrong. (I admit I find his allegation lacking – who has ever seen an alligator wear a top hat?)

In fact, he has become the prime example of someone who takes to the INTER-LOGS solely to irritate and cajole others by spreading misinformation. Who would take delight in such a thing? Such an individual should be banished to live under a bridge!

Before I fell asleep, I began working on a new term for the thing people do when they boast about something admirable they have done while pretending to have a scintilla of humility. It's at the tips of my fingers, and I will report back when I think of it. Although, when the perfect phrase comes to me, I will no doubt humbly brag about it!

June 11, 1916

The streets of Chicago this week have seen the largest parade in this nation's history, the formation of America's first women's political party, and the nomination of the man who will surely become the next president of the United States.

But all of these events pale in comparison to the events of last night.

It all began just prior to the Wednesday morning opening of the Republican National Convention. On Tuesday night, fistfights broke out in hotels all over town, with competing bands of candidate loyalists duking it out in public. At the Congress Hotel, a fight between Teddy Roosevelt supporters and those loyal to Illinois Senator Lawrence Sherman went on for a half hour, continuing a skirmish that had begun earlier in the day. (The local paper said the second fight made the first one look like a "pacifist sewing circle.")

The two major men's conventions – Republican and Progressive –have brought trainloads of what the local paper called "crude men and stylish women" from far states. The women wore gay summer gowns – "cut high enough to reveal a glimpse of silken ankles" – and followed "Negroes of portentous solemnity, who stopped now and then to shake hands with white political managers whose cordiality seemed a trifle forced."

In fact, with the two major men's conventions running concurrently, Chicago has seen an overflow of men desperate for companionship during the week's after-hours festivities. After the first night of the parties, the mayor's entertainment committee made a frantic appeal for ladies to come to the city to ply the men with late-night relationships.

"The downtown hotels report that they have hosts of men, but few to dance with them," said Harry Fowler, chairman of the subcommittee on programs. "We particularly want the suffragists who showed their pluck by marching today. We want Progressive women, and everybody."

To which, the convention goers released the following statement: "Let's not get crazy."

It was only on Tuesday that Justice Charles Evans Hughes made his first public statement, finally admitting he may be interested in seeking the presidency. He even gave his not-yet-official campaign a slogan, which will surely be used for noble means in the future of this nation's politics: America First!

As the convention opened, the five major planks of the Republican Party's platform were unveiled: Preparedness, Peace, Americanism, Tariffs, and Mexico. The floor of the convention was chaotic, as the decision to bar Teddy Roosevelt from the proceedings angered TR's supporters (and likely led to the fistfights in which they frequently engaged.)

Of course, even physically barred from the convention, Teddy Roosevelt is casting a significant shadow over the process. If Republicans continue to block him, TR has threatened to walk down the street and seek the nomination of the progressive Bull Moose Party. If he were to do that, he would undoubtedly sink any chance a Republican would have of beating Woodrow Wilson in November, as the non-Democratic vote would be split as is was in 1912 when Roosevelt ran and handed Wilson the White House.

But, at the first meeting of the Women's Party conference held just across the street, the famous Helen Keller warned the Republican Party to not support TR in his quest for the presidency, calling him "the most to be feared man in the United States today." It is true; since he relinquished the presidency, TR has been prone to even more intemperate and boisterous comments. How could America ever elect anyone other than an upstanding gentleman with an unshakeable demeanor?

Back at the GOP convention, supporters of eleven different men argued in favor of their preferred candidates. Hughes appeared to be the frontrunner, although even the indecisive justice himself was condemned, as cries of "Never Hughes!" rained down on the delegates.

The convention floor itself was a wild scene, with one woman dressed in an American flag and waving a red parasol screaming for TR until she passed out in the aisle. One delegate named Shaw contracted the "jumping Methodist" fever, hopping up and down and swinging his arms wildly until he was subdued by police officers.

Yet the true subterfuge was taking place every night after the sweltering, cavernous Coliseum cleared out and delegates made their way to the balls being held at fourteen hotels around the city.

Last night, Dirk and yours truly found ourselves at a dance held by the Congress Hotel. If journalists are known for anything, it is their dedication to free food – so, before the crowd really filed in, my companion and I grabbed some small plates of mini-sausages, two whiskeys, and began to make small-talk.

"Notice anything a little odd about the attendees here?" he asked.

Squinting my eyes and surveying the room, I noticed a great number of the men in attendance were sporting voluptuous beards.

"There appears to be a great deal of facial hair in the room," I said. "Have we stumbled upon a reception for either bohemians, lumberjacks, or federal witnesses?"

He explained that, for each notable delegate in the room, several private investigators had been hired to follow them. Basically, every sleuth in America had been put on the candidates' payrolls and had been sent out to gather incriminating information on the candidates and their delegates.

This situation set up quite a spiral of intrigue. For instance, candidate X would hire a private dick to follow candidate Y. But candidate Y would then not only hire a detective to follow candidate X, he would hire another investigator to follow the private detective hired to follow HIM. (And, as you can guess, the detective agency would hire another detective to follow the detective hired to follow the original detective.)

And, in a feeble attempt to keep all their identities secret, each of them had adopted preposterous chin toupees.

"Must be a good time for cheating wives," I heard a voice say behind me, as Dirk finished up his explanation. I turned and saw a tall, impeccably dressed man approach me.

"Bernard Wolfe," he said, reaching his hand out to shake mine. "I'm a delegate from Michigan."

"Nice to meet you. Although I admit, I'm not sure I know what you're talking about," I told him.

"Well, do the math, friend," he said, nestling up next to Dirk and me. "Most private investigators are hired by men to follow their unfaithful wives around. And virtually every private detective in the nation is currently in this four-block radius. So, there's not a lot of surveillance happening on America's streets," he said.

"The cuckold patrol has been redeployed," I said.

"Exactly," said Bernard. "I imagine a great number of delegates will be returning home from the convention in several days to wives that will be having babies that look suspiciously like the town bicycle salesman in nine months."

"It's not like the men aren't here having their own fun," said Dirk.

"Not me," said Bernard. "I brought my wife along, so I must behave."

I noticed three hirsute men about ten feet away scribbling furiously in notebooks.

"Some people think it's loony to bring your wife to a national convention," he said. "Like it's bringing a Christmas ham with you to a steak dinner. But she's quite sharp politically," he said. "She loathes this new brand of insistent progressive woman."

"Well, you may not be allowed to have any fun, but I plan on making my last night here memorable," I said. I decided to try out my newly minted catch-phrase, "Please hold my beer while I leave you temporarily to do something inadvisable."

Just then, over Wolfe's left shoulder, I saw a woman with her back to us whip her head around and look directly at me. She turned around and stood, eyes fixed directly on yours truly. Perhaps she had seen me at the women's parade several weeks before and recognized me; my instinct was to immediately flee.

But I also couldn't stop looking at her. She was dressed in the finest pink silk gown, her brown hair tucked neatly into an exquisite wide-brimmed hat. Describing her beauty could fill volumes penned by the most adept romantic poet; I immediately wished I had an extra set of eyes to be able to take in all of her radiance at once.

She began to walk toward our conversational triumvirate. I began to perspire as if I had just robbed an orphanage. A woman that looks like her typically wouldn't even talk to me to warn me that a moose was falling from the sky and about to land on me.

"Oh hello, honey," Wolfe said to her, as she approached. "Good fellows, this is my wife, Grace."

"Hello," she said.

"These two men work at a newspaper in Milwaukee, here to cover the big convention," Wolfe said.

Her eyes got a little wider. I started to become very self-conscious. I was beginning to think I had actually grown those two extra eyes for which I had previously wished.

"I think I just heard something about Milwaukee in the news," she said, smiling. "Wasn't there a woman's parade that was ruined by some local imbecile trying to impress a lady?"

My dry mouth opened and words fell out. "Uh, I don't recall seeing anything about that," I said.

"I think my friend Virginia told me about it," she said. "She lives there."

I have never been a proponent of murder, but if someone in the room pulled out a pistol, shot a rival, and the room erupted in chaos, it would be worth it to get me out of this conversation.

"You didn't tell me you had any friends in Milwaukee, sweetie," said Bernard. "Maybe these two know her."

"I don't think so," I said, contemplating whether it would be wise to pull my jacket over my head.

"She was telling me about this silly man trying to start a business selling shirts with only sleeves," she said, now wearing the grin of someone holding the world's best secret. The realization hit me as if I had just been slapped in the face by a flounder.

"Exactly where again did you say you were from in Michigan?" I asked Wolfe.

"Kalamazoo," he said.

I stood silent, my senses dull and my brain numb. Bernard and Dirk exchanged some tidbits about Michigan politics. I looked at her and smiled. She now knew I knew what she knew. I was looking at WillieCat.

Suddenly, I didn't know what to say. Standing in front of me was one of my best friends, with whom I had spent hours upon hours talking. And yet, with one (albeit major) revelation, I had no idea what to say to her.

In one sense, I was stunned at the statistical probability that we would be in the same city at the same time and actually be in a situation to find one another, given we were both, in theory, anonymous.

But her otherworldly beauty also immediately became a problem. I was never particularly skilled at talking to pretty women – my tongue would swell as if stung by bees that had all just been told they were adopted. I was much better typing my thoughts. I could muster up "keystroke courage" to say what I wanted in the comfort of my own home and wished I was there now to properly express my feelings. (Although I knew I would have to block her from seeing my public posts, which I have obviously done for this one. Clearly, it will be impossible for her to see!)

And yet, I couldn't help but think of the wickedness of it all. Here was the ideal woman of whom I had always dreamed. She was preternaturally comely, smart, and funny. She knew all my most intimate secrets. She shared laughs with me when I told her of all my awkward adventures. And, through it all, she still actually seemed to like me.

But she was married. To Bernard. Wealthy investment banker

Bernard. The politician.

It seemed like one of those Biblical tests I read about as a child. It was as if God had placed this cruel conundrum before me to see if I could control myself. Even though I felt as if I should quit my job to be able to spend more time thinking about her, she was already betrothed. Perhaps, like Lot's wife, if I failed this test I would be turned into a pillar of salt.

I had no intention of becoming a common table seasoning, so I pulled myself together.

Just then, a man ran into the room waving a piece of piece of paper while commanding everyone to be silent. "I've just received word from my people at the Coliseum," he said. "Colonel Roosevelt was just nominated on the second ballot by a margin of seven hundred!" he yelled.

A confused Dirk and Bernard looked at one another, believing they had missed the final vote.

"Wait here, honey bear," Wolfe said, presumably talking to Grace. He and Dirk ran out of the room to see what had happened.

With the coast all clear, I turned to WillieCat. "You don't really know Virginia, do you?"

"Of course not," she laughed. "I respected you enough to try to get that hint."

"How did you know it was me?" I said.

"That stupid catchphrase of yours really needs some work," she said. "Any other sane human in the world would have trimmed it by now."

We began walking toward the lobby to see whether the commotion over the final vote was justified. As we took a few steps forward, I saw a false beard and a notebook on the ground and picked them up; presumably, a private detective dropped them on the sprint to the door.

I put the book in my back pocket and handed her the beard. "I think you need to wear this, 'Willie,'" I said, mimicking quotation marks with my fingers. She playfully elbowed me in the ribs.

Just then, Dirk and Bernard, both out of breath, walked back into the room.

"The man totally made it up," said Wolfe. "So the crowd beat him senseless."

Consider that man's well-being a sacrifice made for me, as I was able to spend a few invaluable minutes conversing with the world's most stunning, and least available, woman.

"Let's go," Wolfe said, motioning to his wife. "We have to make an appearance at the governor's reception at nine."

"Goodbye, Sebastian," she said, extending her hand.

"Goodbye, Grace."

July 1, 1916

The days following my return home were filled with confusion and malaise. I continued to talk to WillieCat through direct messages, but our conversations suddenly shifted. I had to be more careful and polite about what I said, as my words were reaching the delicate eyeballs of a lady!

She apologized endlessly about leading me to believe she was a brother in manhood. She said she enjoyed our conversations so much, she knew they would change if her gender was revealed. She hadn't planned on making such good friends on the FINGER-PHONE, and, if she had, she would have revealed all much earlier. Plus, the chances of us actually meeting in person were about the same as a presidential candidate mentioning his genitalia during a campaign debate – zero!

Even though we were still able to talk secretly, my overall disposition became surly and irritable. This was, in large part, because we were able to continue conversing.

For instance, when we weren't messaging back and forth, I would begin to worry why it had been a full day since she responded to one of my searing witticisms. It seems before the FINGER-PHONE, I didn't care whether someone else was thinking about me at any given moment, because there was no way for that other person to contact me and confirm it. If they went through a full day, and I failed to enter their thoughts, I wouldn't know it.

But now, I feel like every minute WillieCat isn't sending me a message, she is making a conscious choice to deny me her company. Now that I know she could be messaging me at any time, I become dyspeptic when she isn't. The human mind was more peaceful when you knew your friends couldn't just contact you at any time!

It also rankles yours truly that I only end up talking to WillieCat when I initiate the conversation. When we do share our thoughts with one another, it is glorious. But it is clear that if I didn't make the choice to message her, we would never speak again.

Is this some form of universally accepted modern-day chivalry? Like holding a door open, or taking a bite out of a woman's piece of chicken before she gets to eat it to make sure it hasn't been poisoned. Must the man initiate contact every time?

I had many of these questions on my mind as Basil and I sat at the Spotted Oyster a week following my return. He is the person I trust most with my innermost thoughts, so I provided him with some information that would be too sensitive for even a U.S. president to know.

"I have to make an impossible choice," I told him. "Do I pursue the woman close to me who continues in her belief that I am a buffoon, or do I hold out hope for a married woman across Lake Michigan who is clearly my soulmate?"

"Who is this lucky lady in town?" he asked.

When I told him it was Virginia, he spit out his martini.

"Doesn't she already have a male suitor?" he asked, clearly amused by my revelation.

"Yes, but he's a sop," I said. "I just need to demonstrate my all-around excellence and I can wrest her from the clutches of that cursed Bertrand."

"One would think she would have seen deep into your soul by now," he said, patting his silk vest.

"Wait, you're not trying to steal her, are you?" I asked. For some reason, he sighed, closed his eyes, and shook his head.

"No, she's all yours," he said.

"It would seem that she is your only viable option at this point, given this Grace woman is very far away and very married," he added.

"That's the thing," I said, slowly pulling out a small brown notebook from my pocket. "At the convention in Chicago, her husband was being tailed by a cadre of private investigators, and I found this on the floor." I showed him the notebook that had been dropped by one of the detectives.

The pages were full of sordid actions alleged to have been taken by Michigan delegate Bernard Wolfe over the past several years. On the sixth page, it alleged that he had masterminded a plot to sell illicit oleomargarine. According to the charge, Wolfe had funded an underground ring of criminals who had been applying yellow color to oleomargarine and selling it as butter – one of the nation's most scandalous of crimes!

On the tenth page, the notebook detailed a 1914 scam in which Wolfe wrote a book called How to Make a Million Dollars for Dummies, but the book was simply one page that said, "Write a $1 book on how to make a million dollars and sell a million copies."

But the most shocking charge was found on page fourteen, where it mentioned Wolfe was seen at the convention engaging in a clandestine meeting with another man at his Chicago apartment. Evidently, Bernard was able to slip away from WillieCat long enough to partake in what the notebook called "Oscar Wilde-style activities." And I don't think it meant penning whimsical reflections on age and beauty!

When I told Basil about this unnatural union, his interest was piqued.

"Maybe I should go pay this Bernard a visit," he said.

While I told him it was very kind of him to offer to defend the honor of lovely Grace, I told him he should do no physical harm to Bernard Wolfe. Basil was, after all, very tall and fit for a man of whatever undetermined age he may be and could likely injure delegate Wolfe with the most minimal of effort.

"I forbid you from pounding him," I ordered my chivalrous friend.

"Sounds like the best-case scenario," he retorted, eyebrows raised.

Kind soul that he is, Basil offered me an emotional salve for my troubles with the opposite sex. He told me it would be best to keep the news of Mr. Bernard Wolfe to myself, as these types of things tend to work themselves out over time. That is why I am only sharing it with my best friends on the FINGER-PHONE – I assume you will all keep this secret.

"Sadly, I suspect this woman in Michigan is too large of an elephant for you to mount," he said. "You need to take better care of yourself so Virginia can see the beauty inside you."

"There's nothing ladies like better than confidence," Basil told me. "For the love of God, some poor woman even married that walrus Otto and had children with him. It's because he doesn't know he shouldn't have any confidence."

"I'm not sure any amount of confidence I could have can erase my boobery in Virginia's presence," I said.

"Well you have to start somewhere," he said. "If you don't have any self-esteem, you should take steps to turn that around. Show her you are immaculate in hygiene, dress, manners, and education," he said.

"I think my dress and manners are just fine," I said, noting that I rarely wore the same shirt for more than three days consecutively. Further, the salesman at the drug store told me the pig's feet-scented moustache wax he sold me was the pinnacle of aphrodisiacs.

"Darling, your look is busted," Basil said, patting me on the back in the reassuring way a mother might do to a child to whom she is breaking the news about the Tooth Fairy's origins.

"But, I can help you," he said. "It just so happens I am starting a new service where I and four of my friends come to your house and give you a one-night course in dress, culture, cooking, and interior design."

"What a queer idea!" I said.

"Indeed, there is nothing else like it in the city," he said. "And it is only thirty dollars."

I nearly choked on my Duff's whiskey.

"Thirty dollars?" I yelped. "That's a full two weeks' pay!"

"Do you want to unlock your inner self or not?" Basil said.

"Okay, fine," I relented. "But if Virginia and I are not soulmates within one week, I will send delegate Bernard Wolfe to our hometown to wrestle you to the ground!" I said.

"I think that can be arranged," he said.

When I appeared at my work desk the next morning, I was greeted with stories of other lovelorn souls that may be even direr than mine.

Last weekend, a man named Joseph A. Thomas was married in Milwaukee. Only, in Chicago, police were investigating Thomas' poisoning of his previous wife with cyanide.

Sadly, poisonings have become all too common in unhappy marriages. The leading cause of death among married women is "wandering husband." The divorce laws are prohibitive; in order for a man to be granted a divorce, he must prove infidelity on the part of his wife. In order for a woman to be granted a divorce from her husband, she must prove that her husband was unfaithful, beat her, murdered her, burned her body, and urinated on the ashes – only then would her divorce request finally be granted.

In the Thomas case, the victim's sister said the deceased had told her Thomas had tried to poison her several times before.

Indeed, her interest was piqued the sixth time, when he baked her cyanide chip cookies. Jeweler A. Engleman said Thomas came to him asking for cyanide to kill his sick dog, but Engleman rebuffed him, noting that he had no dog. An embarrassed Thomas then said it was actually for poisoning a dolphin that had been making threats against his family. "Well, in that case," Engleman said, knowing how dolphins can be.

Marital unrest also struck Frank Duquay and his wife Carrie Turriff. Back in October, while an inmate in county jail, Duquay unsuccessfully attempted to hang himself. Following that incident, Duquay wrote to the city's mayor under an assumed name, asking the mayor to help him find a wife. This sparked intense media coverage, and Miss Turriff answered Duquay's call, marrying him within days of meeting him.

Turriff then gave Duquay the amount of $1,700 in order to open a grocery store in Chicago. But Turriff is now suing her husband for embezzlement, saying the store was never opened. What kind of world is it when you can't trust someone who tries to hang himself and seeks a wife based on the publicity it garners? Bring back the old days, I say!

On Monday, a man posing as an expert in electrical safe security for banks snatched up a large bag of money from a vault he was allowed to "inspect" and jumped through a plate glass window at St. Anthony's bank. The bank's clerical staff was able to catch the man and hold him to the ground for two minutes before a police officer happened to walk by and arrest the perpetrator. As it turns out, however, the police officer was also an actor, and the two happily split the money. Perhaps they deposited it at St. Anthony's bank, knowing how well the safe works!

A recent story I typed for the Post detailed all of the odd automobile license numbers being requested by society's elite car-owners. Our United States Senator, Robert M. La Follette, requested license tag No. 1 but was rejected and given No. 2. It turns out that Madison grocer John G. Hyland beat the senator's application by mere minutes and then renamed his grocery "Hyland's No. 1" in honor of his feat.

Nonetheless, over 1,000 requests are made per year for license No. 1 from those not knowing it has already been issued. Over fifty requests are made annually for those tempting fate and wanting unlucky No. 13. One man requested a plate made up entirely from the numbers three and eight, thinking police wouldn't be able to read the numbers as he sped by. I fully agree that the city's maximum speed limit of eight miles per hour is unduly restrictive!

Curiously, over four hundred requests per year are made for the No. 69. As I typed this fact out, I asked out loud why this might be the case. "You'll see," said Philly, chortling.

I had no time for japery, however, as Basil and his fabulous four friends were due to show up at my house within the hour.

Shortly after six, all five gentlemen appeared at my front door, accompanied by a photographer for some reason.

"Why are you documenting this?" I asked Basil.

"Just some publicity photos," he said, "to get business going."

Despite my initial misgivings, I had the most delightful time! Each of Basil's chums was so full of mirth and good humor – what I wouldn't give to belong to any club where I could enjoy their company all the time!

First, a good-smelling young man named Maurice gave me a haircut and trimmed my moustache, all the while using phrases such as "Slay, queen"; I don't know quite what it meant, but I'm certain yelling such a thing could get you arrested on the streets of merry old England!

A blonde man in his early twenties named Clarence taught me how to make something called an "appetizer" with a new fruit called the "alligator pear." (Last year, it was renamed the "avocado," but that name evidently has not yet caught on.)

An even younger man named Jeremy taught me some of the youthful songs of the day, including, "Oh! How She Could Yacki, Hacki, Wicki, Wacki, Woo," "Take Me Back to Dear Old Blighty," and the aptly named "I'm Gonna Make Hay While the Sun Shines in Virginia."

Meanwhile, Basil stood in my bedroom and fretted over my wardrobe. While I am not anyone's vision of sartorial splendor, my clothes are perfectly functional; my two pairs of trousers, three button-down shirts, vest, and three neckties are just enough to allow me to leave the house without having vegetables thrown at me. Indeed, the idea of wearing something that calls attention to myself gives me the chills!

"No, no, no," my chum counseled me. "This will not do at all. We need to make you more 'fashion-forward.'"

He began pulling clothing accessories out of a satchel he had brought with him. First, he handed me a purple and blue scarf and told me to tie it around my neck.

"Absolutely not!" I shrieked.

Then, he handed me a small hat with a stiff awning in front, similar to those worn by baseball players.

"Who in their right mind would ever wear sports clothes in public?" I said.

"Okay, this is your final chance," Basil cautioned.

Out of his bag, he pulled what appeared to be a large, circular Shakespearean-era ruffled collar. It appeared to be about three feet in diameter and nearly six inches thick.

"I didn't pay you thirty dollars to make jokes," I told Basil. "Evidently, you have mistaken me for a Tudor."

"I have read that, in Portugal, eligible young men are fighting each other for these," said Basil. "We all know styles eventually come back around, and you could be on the razor's edge of this trend," he said. "The ruff is a statement that you are your own man and play your own vigilante rules of fashion."

"It is a statement that I wish to die alone," I said.

"Nonsense!" he said. "What could be more attractive to a lady than a man so confident in himself that he is willing to step outside of his own realm of comfort? What woman can resist a chap willing to defy the conventions of society to live his own truth? Aren't you willing to make this one small change to unlock the vast possibilities in your future?"

"At least, if Virginia doesn't go on a date with me, I can now have her beheaded," I said.

As I tried on the giant ruffled collar, I saw a blinding flash from the camera. I handed Basil his thirty dollars, and they all embraced me and headed to the door. Young Clarence looked over his shoulder and called me "fierce," which I believe is a bit unfair as I was perfectly friendly with every one of them.

As I sat alone on my bed, I knew if I didn't take Basil's advice I would have wasted two weeks' worth of my meager salary. Clearly, he knew what he was doing; he always had so many attractive lady-friends willing to spend time with him and tell him all their problems. If wearing Renaissance-era garb and eating alligator pears was the cost of my entry into the world of the city's art scene, I must make it happen!

The next morning, I woke, took a bath, and scrubbed my face with a special blend of oatmeal and honey the boys had provided me. Evidently, it is a part of my new regimen of "self-care."

I dressed as normal, put my new fashion accessory in a burlap sack, and walked out the door. When I entered the Milwaukee Post, I immediately headed for the men's lavatory to strap on my new cloth mane.

As I walked down the hall to the stairs, everyone stopped in their tracks when they saw me. Clearly, they had never laid eyes on a man so uncompromising in his style!

As I made my way down the stairs to the typing room, I quickly eyed the territory to see what reaction I would get. When Philly saw me, he immediately stopped talking, which is a Herculean feat in and of itself. Otto, who had his back to me, sensed something was afoot when he heard Philly cut off his sentence and wheeled around to feast his eyes on my fashion triumph.

I settled into my seat and began typing my first story of the day, although I had to lean forward at a forty-five degree angle to be able to see the keyboard in front of me. In Reading, Pennsylvania, a house was set ablaze when a goat began chewing a pair of trousers that had matches in the pocket. Thankfully, everyone escaped the fire alive, and it was deemed an accident – until police discovered that the goat had taken out an insurance policy on the premises a week ago!

Just then, I saw a feminine figure walk up beside me to my left. As Virginia sat down at her LinoType, I could feel her eyes on me, and I began to sweat profusely. I stared straight ahead and continued to hammer away at the keyboard, intending to send her the message that her attention was not important to me.

After about six excruciating minutes of her staring at me (undoubtedly admiring my sartorial flair). I felt her put her hand on my shoulder.

This was it! She was about to succumb to my undeniable manliness!

"Dear," she said softly.

"Yes?" I answered, turning to her in anticipation of her whispers of love.

"If you lost a bet, I would be happy to pay off the debt for you," she said. "Who put you up to this? Is this a condition of your parole?"

It seemed that the discussion had taken quite a turn. I jolted from my seat, ripped off the sweat-soaked collar, and sprinted up the stairs – while Philly's boisterous laughs echoed in my ears.

I ran all the way home, slammed the door shut, and slumped to the floor. After several minutes of wiping tears from my moustache, I began to feel better. At least I hadn't worn that baseball cap in public!

July 15, 1916

Having taken several days to restore my standing at work, I walked to the newspaper slowly on Monday, dreading having to face Virginia and the band of taunting jackals in the typing room. It was a warm morning, and I wanted to take as long as I could to get there. So I stopped in front of a ribbon-cutting ceremony at City Hall.

Recently, the mayor had held a contest to rename the historic building. To give the contest the dignity afforded an honest democratic process, the mayor allowed an open vote from citizens of Milwaukee to choose the name.

As he stood in front of the majestic building, he pulled out an envelope and announced the new name was contained within.

"And forevermore, City Hall will be known as..."

He paused as flashbulbs crackled around him.

"Buildy McBuildingface!" he yelled.

The announcement was met with dead silence until, around a minute later, a teenage boy yelled "HURRAY!" before running away. As he ran, small slips of paper fell from a bag hung around his neck. I picked one up and it looked suspiciously like a ballot – undoubtedly this young scamp had stuffed the voting box!

I have continued speaking online to my beloved Grace, keeping any of my secret information to myself. Even when we are not messaging back and forth between ourselves, I find myself daydreaming about her, wondering if she were packing her bags that moment to move to Milwaukee and jump into my arms.

But I also suspect I would be much happier had I never learned the secret of her gender. After all, she is forbidden, having given herself to another man for life. I often feel the effects of this barrier as if I had swallowed a cannonball whole. In a sense, she has given me a glimpse of what my life could be, but never will. I certainly would be happier had I never known someone of her caliber was out there in the world!

Suppose for a moment you had a family dog to whom, for years, you had fed only table scraps and dry canine food. What a happy dog little Petey would be! But then, one day, Petey finds himself in possession of a most tender ribeye steak, marbled with delicious fat!

Before he even finished devouring this succulent treat, Petey would immediately recognize the food you had been feeding him his entire life was complete garbage. Now that he knew the ceiling for food was much higher than what he had been accustomed to, he would be consistently grouchy and irritable, unwilling to settle for less. "Feed me a chateaubriand with plenty of pink!" he would yell at you, throwing his dry kibbles at your head.

And you'd be so angry, you'd forget the fact that your dog knew how to speak!

I have heard there is nothing women enjoy more than being compared to cuts of meat, so I will admit I am Petey the dog in this scenario and Grace is the gold standard of beef. Only, in this metaphorical world, there is only one butcher and, if I came near his product, he would likely sever all my limbs from my body.

It has thusly occurred to me that if food were love, I would be a pile of bones resting on the side of an empty alleyway. An emaciated carcass picked clean by the vultures of romance. I have heard researchers at Johns Hopkins medical school in Baltimore have developed a new serum that will revive any corpse within four hours of death – yet I can only be revived by one serum, and it is named "WillieCat."

With this realization, I glumly dragged myself to work on Tuesday, not wanting to talk to anyone. I saw Virginia at her machine and quickly shuffled, undetected, to the row behind her. It was at that point that I saw poor Otto sitting at his desk, wearing what appeared to be a fez with a cord running from the top of the hat into the wall.

Seeing this queer sight, I had to break my silence and ask Otto what in the name of all-that-is-cream-of-wheat was he doing.

Otto had recently instituted a "points rule" for use in the office. His workmates were only allowed to speak to him if they had accumulated enough "points" for him to deem them worthy of conversation. These points were granted solely by him and for whatever reason he saw fit, but complimenting him was typically the best way to earn credits.

"You don't have enough points to ask me that question," he said.

"How many points short am I?" I asked.

"You don't have enough points to ask me that question," he said.

Not having expected to join him in conversation at all, I was unable to hide my irritation.

"I've seen the way you eat, and you should be much fatter than you are, Otto," I said, thinking of the nicest compliment I could possibly pay him.

"Three points," he said. "State your query."

"Why are you running an electric current through your head?" I asked.

He explained that his electric fez was meant to use a current to stimulate his scalp and thus regrow the hair on his shiny dome. This certainly seemed to be a case of a wish being the father of the thought, but what harm could it really do?

He said he couldn't afford the more expensive version that shocked the head with more wattage, so he hadn't seen any results yet but the company guaranteed he would start to see hair within six months. I asked him when the latest date was that he could return the contraption to get his money back.

"Five months," he said.

I should note that, given his generally poor health, portly midsection, and overall misanthropic attitude, Otto is a voracious consumer of any and all recent scientific cures. And it is good that these new types of medicines and procedures are currently flooding America's homes. According to a recent article in Collier's magazine, nearly half of all the ad revenue taken in by newspapers in America is for patent medicines.

Oftentimes, the advertisements are disguised as news stories so the reader cannot distinguish between a vigorously reported article and a paid product placement. In fact, today's paper included a news story-looking piece singing the praises of Humphrey's Homeopathic Remedies, which it is claimed has been healing people for nearly sixty years!

Among the afflictions Humphrey's guarantees to cure:

- Fevers, congestions, inflammations

- Toothache, headache

- Crying infants

- Sweaty eyeballs

- Too many eyeballs

- Disappearing butthole

- Bad at geography

- Death (only up to seven days)

- Webbed feet

- Grumpy wiener

- Ghosts loudly cutting fingernails

- Husband thinks he's a pelican

- Constantly interrupting award winners at award shows

- Wife is a pelican

- Hallucinating about future black president

- Nickelback

- Wanted pregnancy

- And finally, too much disposable income

All those problems eliminated with one pill! It seems too good to be true! But, if these companies have enough money to spend so lavishly on advertisements, customers must be purchasing their product again and again, having experienced dramatic results.

However, my impeccable colleague Mr. Basil Featherstone thinks it is all, to use his word, "quackery." He has noted that eighty percent of all physical afflictions heal themselves eventually if nothing at all is done, so these pharmaceuticals may be taking credit for the body's natural process. Plus, Basil noted what French pharmacist Émile Coué has come to call the "placebo effect," whereby people simply feel better by thinking they are receiving treatment for an affliction.

Further, Basil read that many of the "doctors" that endorse these products have had no medical training and only receive credentials by paying for them. According to one study, there are currently 25,000 "doctors" practicing in America whose degree came with no training whatsoever!

At first, I thought this statistic to be absurd. Yet I do admit I thought it a bit queer when I received my last rectal exam from my neighborhood tobacconist. Although he was insistent and very thorough, it seems slightly odd that he accepted payment in hugs...

Nonetheless, such medicinal schemes promise to bring youth and vitality to the aged and broken. The lengths to which humans are willing to go to regain their youth is legendary; in the fifteenth century, Pope Innocent VII even sought to revivify himself by drinking the blood of young boys. And now, one doctor has promised to restore virility to men by implanting them with the testicles from young goats.

While undoubtedly sound medicine, the goat gland procedure has sparked a debate across the land. The Chicago Federation of Labor has objected - noting that if infertile men could now reproduce, it would mean more child labor to supplant union workers in the factories. At a recent Manhattan literary symposium, poets gathered to protest the goat testicle procedure and the longer life spans it promises to bring. When poets no longer fear death, what else will there be about which to write introspective pentameter?

In this week's news, there was a great deal of macabre health goings-on. At a recent hearing of the U.S. Senate's health committee, doctors testified that over five hundred lepers are currently "at large" in America, constituting a "menace." To me, this seems to be an overstatement - if someone has a disease, they are not "at large" in the sense that a bank robber is. In fact, if they have leprosy, they are more likely to leave you with something than take from you. Yet, the Senate committee has endorsed segregation of these unfortunates, advocating construction of a national "leprosarium."

At the University of Wisconsin in Madison, medical school professor H.C. Bradley gave a speech on Wednesday in which he extolled the nutritional virtues of cannibalism. Again, using the most rigorous of research techniques granted him by university funding, Bradley said the "ideal food would be man flesh" and other meats are indigestible when compared to "human steak."

However, one of Bradley's skeptical students snuck behind him during his lecture and managed to rip Bradley's moustache off, revealing the professor as a cow! Bradley immediately escaped – it is rumored the erstwhile doctor is now masquerading as an accountant in Dothan, Alabama.

On Friday, Mr. Norman Kollinski was sentenced to two years in prison for being what a judge called "the laziest man in the city." Kollinski's wife Jennie said her husband was making good wages but was so fond of sleeping that he lost his job. Kollinski then claimed he was "in business for himself," which entailed sleeping until nine o'clock in the morning, waking up, taking his daily constitutional, eating breakfast, and then taking a nap.

When a probation officer visited the Kollinski home, he found the family's five children poorly clothed and "half-starved." In court, Mr. Kollinski disputed this characterization. "I prefer to be an optimist, your honor," Kollinski said. "I like to think of them as half-FED."

In order to punish Kollinski for his eternal somnolence, Judge Backus sentenced him to one year in the house of correction "to take the laziness out of" the man. Of course, if anything will teach a man to support his family, it will be to take him away from his children for a year!

On Thursday night, before I tucked myself into bed, I heard the most boisterous knocking at my door. As I turned the knob to ascertain who was making such a racket, the door flung open and there stood my old college roommate, Mr. Boomer Mills.

"Good evening, dear Sebastian!" he bellowed.

"Oh, hullo," I answered, about as happy to see him as one would be to see a dead mouse in his potato stew.

"Going to bed so early?" he asked, pushing his way into my home and resting uncomfortably on the only small, wooden chair I had in my living room.

"It's been a long week already," I told him. "Thought a bit of shuteye might bring me back to life."

"Worry not," he said, jolting to a standing position. "I have just the thing that will re-energize your flaccid soul," he said.

Trying hard to prevent my eyes from rolling out of my head, I asked him what this emotional elixir might comprise.

"You will feel better about yourself merely by knowing you fulfilled your end of the bargain with me," he said.

I knew what this was about. In exchange for not embarrassing me at the ladies' parade, I had agreed to run a notice in the newspaper for him.

He reached into his coat pocket, pulled out a small piece of paper, and handed it to me.

It read:

MILWAUKEE SOCIETY PAYS HANDSOMELY TO MEET NORWEGIAN ROYALTY

Enthusiastic members of the city's societal elite have paid top dollar to attend a ball to welcome Duke Rudolf von Biarnex of Norway, who is considering relocating in

Milwaukee. Duke Rudolf, a man of considerable wealth and eighteenth in line to the Norwegian throne, says he is very much interested in finding female companionship during his time in the city. Potential suitors among Milwaukee's upper class have been paying fifty dollars a ticket to attend the ball in his honor on August 28 at the Pabst Ballroom.

"What in Genghis Khan's underwear is this?" I asked.

"Don't worry about it. Just run it," he said.

"'Biarnex' doesn't sound very Norwegian," I answered.

"It's not your concern. It's a lesser-known branch of the royal family," he shot back.

"And I'm pretty sure they don't have dukes in Norway."

"I cordially invite you to go have intercourse with yourself," he said, utilizing a phrase he believes he invented. "Are you the goddamned Encyclopedia Britannica now?"

"What's this all about?" I asked.

"I met this fellow on my world travels," he said. "He's Norwegian royalty but loves American moving pictures, so he wanted to come here and meet his own movie star. I told him there was no better place to meet a beautiful, wealthy woman than Milwaukee, Wisconsin."

"It all checks out," I said. "I'll do it. This could get me fired, but a Schneider always pays his debts."

"You're a good friend," he said, walking out the door. "The

duke thanks you."

The next day, armed with Boomer's tiny news item, I settled in to my typing machine to make a new plate for printing. It was so small, who could possibly even notice once it was tucked into the thousands of words the Milwaukee Post produced every day?

As soon as I began typing, I could feel a warm sensation on my neck. I wheeled around and saw Basil Featherstone looking over my shoulder.

"What is that you're typing from that ragged piece of paper?" he asked.

"It's just a tiny edit," I said. "One of the cake recipes in the paper accidentally called for three cups of 'flowers' instead of three cups of 'flour,'" I said.

"That seems very silly," he said.

"Very much agreed," I said. "I better hurry up and fix this before people are eating petunias for dessert."

"You have five minutes," he said, walking back to the typesetting press.

I quickly finished off Boomer's unquestionably valid story, took it over to Basil, and pretended to accidentally drop it in the bucket where the plates for all the other stories of the day were kept. I then returned to my station, where I crumpled the brief news item Boomer's story was to replace, then put it in my mouth and swallowed it.

Now nobody would know the original story had been replaced. After all, it was something completely forgettable: German Army

Cartoonist Wounded in Battle, Escapes Death. Some random soldier named "Adolf Hitler" or something.

August 1, 1916

During one of our discussions the other night, WillieCat and I conceived of the most riotous business plan!

Recently, fellow FINGER-PHONE user "StableGenius45" suddenly ceased responding to anyone from his device. This fellow was particularly known for trafficking in ribald material and conspiracy theories (he even suspected ingesting radium was bad for you!) It was later found out that he was an elderly man who had died!

WillieCat was concerned that, once he passed away, he may have all manner of unflattering materials in his home that he had gathered through the anonymous connections he had made through interconnectivity. What would his family think when they went to his home, found him dead, and checked his FINGER-PHONE only to find his most prurient, distasteful secrets laid bare?

To aid just such a situation, Grace and I crafted a detailed plan to provide "reputation insurance" for FINGER-PHONE users who preferred their secrets to go to their grave with them. For a fee, one of our staff members would go to the deceased person's home, dispose of their FINGER-PHONE, and locate the special file where secret documents are held. (Location of this file would be known only to us.)

Take, for example, the Ohio man who was fond of receiving lascivious material on his machine, only to one day accidentally leave such explicit material in the printing box. When his wife sat down to use the FINGER-PHONE, she came upon the dirty tome and shrieked. She immediately ran to her husband, paper in hand, and waved it in front of him.

"It appears our machine has been infected by a 'virus,'" she yelled, referring to certain codes that can be transmitted through phone lines and ruin a FINGER-PHONE's functionality.

"Uh...yes, that is definitely it," he said. Getting right on the case, he purchased a fifty dollar program to "clean" the computer of viruses. He was able to dodge being found out but, without that fifty dollars, his children were not able to wear shoes for the next year.

Thus, imagine all the reputations such a service could preserve! Imagine how many wives would be spared the knowledge of their husbands' late-night activities. Just think of the children, already grief-stricken from the loss of their parent, who would be saved from knowing their father's dark side. And how many kids will be able to have shoes!

As a final service, "Reputation Insurance, Inc." would, when a person assumes room temperature, send out one final FINGER-PHONE post in their name. It is particularly embarrassing when a person's final INTER-LOG statement is something like "LET ME SEE HOW MANY MARBLES I CAN FIT IN MY NOSE" or "I'M GOING TO DRINK A GALLON OF MILK IN FIFTEEN MINUTES." Poor user "SecondChakra's" final post was, "HOLD ON, GUYS, GOING TO GO CHECK TO

SEE WHAT THAT SOUND IN MY BASEMENT IS! BRB!"

Our service would allow a user to leave the world on his terms – leaving his final post as something inspiring, gracious, and humble. Imagine having your final words on earth being something obnoxious someone could read in the year 2018! Who could live on this planet with people knowing you uttered things like "Abraham Lincoln isn't a hero. I like presidents who don't get shot"? Such a person would surely be cast from polite society!

Undoubtedly, Grace and I will one day live together off of our millions we make from this idea. In the weeks since our meeting in Chicago, my admiration for her has only deepened, although I suspect that may be a byproduct of her exterior beauty making me feel as though I had inhaled an entire bag full of ether.

This has caused me to question whether my enthusiasm for her intellectual talents is warranted. Is she legitimately funny and insightful, or am I choosing to believe she is gifted in those areas because she also happens to be preternaturally gorgeous? Would I laugh at her jokes so enthusiastically if she looked like Ulysses S. Grant? What if we really aren't that compatible and I am tricking myself into believing so because of my desire to one day hold her in my arms? After all, I have long felt the most attractive feature in a woman is simply the ability to tolerate me.

Such concerns have been less important, however, as the presidential race has begun in earnest. The presses at my newspaper have been working overtime as President Woodrow Wilson recently, in arguing for America to stay out of the European war, made the preposterous declaration that it is possible for a country to be "too proud to fight."

Yet, with a large number of patriotic Americans in favor of

preparedness, Wilson has faced backlash for his anti-war positions. Republican nominee Charles Evans Hughes has been attacking Wilson on both his weak position on preparedness and his inability to protect American citizens currently residing in Europe.

Wilson's weakness has only been reinforced by Teddy Roosevelt, who said that instead of "speaking softly and carrying a big stick," Wilson "spoke bombastically and carried a dishrag." In the spirit of Mark Twain's famous character, Hughes supporters have begun referring to the president as "Pudd'nhead Wilson."

Within the world of newspapers, word has gotten around that President Wilson will be willing to take action against any publication that openly dissents from his opinions. This is particularly perilous for the Milwaukee Post, which routinely uncovers many of his hare-brained progressive schemes to sculpt society in a manner he finds more palatable. For instance, Wilson has recently proposed a new tax on incomes over $4,000, a surtax of thirteen percent on incomes over two million dollars, and a large tax on the manufacture of bullets!

Nonetheless, despite working at a newspaper that favored Hughes, Virginia told me she swore allegiance to Wilson.

"When Germany shows up on our shores, you'll wish you voted for Hughes," I told her.

"He is committed to peace," she said, turning away from me to continue typing. "And he will rid this nation of the scourge of intoxicating liquor once and for all."

She pretended she didn't see me roll my eyes.

"Take away our spirits and none of your beloved Democrats will ever win another election," I said. "The word 'progressive' will forever be cursed in American politics," I told her.

She ignored me.

"Plus, Wilson is weak on suffrage," I told her. "He wants states to decide whether women get to vote, and Hughes wants a full constitutional amendment," I said.

This was a true fact. Earlier in the week, Hughes addressed a conference of five hundred women and told them he supported full voting rights for women, while Wilson wanted suffrage to remain an issue for the states to decide. In a critique of Wilson, Hughes had said he was "for women" and not "sex politics."

Despite this betrayal, I still fully support Hughes; politicians say all sorts of things to get elected. It's not like he was promising to build a wall around America to keep immigrants out.

"Well, I'm sure you're very happy about that, given how committed to the cause of suffrage you are," she said acidly, turning to face me. I began turning red, as I had not yet admitted to her that it was indeed me she saw at the suffrage parade that day. It was clear she was delivering me a verbal shiv.

"Suffrage is going to happen whether you cavemen want it or not," she said, turning back to her keyboard. "Regardless of who is elected, the movement will not be denied – even if interlopers try to ruin our parades," she said.

"I...do support suffrage?" I said unconvincingly, surprising even me. Suddenly, Cupid had taken control of my senses, making me say ridiculous things.

It was a declaration made in the thralls of panic. But it is clear that, if I were ever to win her love, I would have to resort to desperate measures to overcome my multiple missteps. Virginia's long memory was bad for both of us. For me, it meant it would be more work to get back in her good graces. For her, it was simply bad for her psyche - long memories mean grudges are never forgotten and slights burn far beyond their expiration date.

"Well, good," she said. "You and your boyfriend Hughes can celebrate the cause of women's rights while you drop bombs all over the innocent ladies of Europe."

I felt that perhaps this discussion did not have its intended effect.

At the Spotted Oyster the next day, I commiserated with Philly about my facile attempt to connect with Virginia's politics.

"Nobody believes Wilson is going to be able to keep us out of war, anyway," I said. "Hughes says he's for neutrality, but everyone knows he's not going to keep us out of Europe. The poor pacifists have nowhere to turn but Wilson, and they're being duped."

"The only reason we're not at war right now is because of a broad," Philly noted.

My young drinking companion never struck me as a voracious reader of the news, but this observation was actually accurate. Last year, when Germany sunk the Lusitania and killed 1,200 people, President Wilson was rendered blind by a fog of love. Even as the Kaiser's aggressions murdered hundreds of Americans, Wilson spent his days writing love letters to the former Edith Galt, who would soon become his wife.

"He chose to make love, not war," I said, proud of my witticism that I feel will definitely someday catch on and which nobody will ever tire of hearing.

"He kept America out of war in order to invade her drawers," he crudely added.

"Yes, I think we all get the picture," I said, despite being the only saloon patron at eleven o'clock on a Saturday morning.

"So you're saying it's crazy to take political stands just to see a woman naked?" he said.

I knew what he was doing.

"You're not funny," I said. "I hate you."

"Why are you getting so worked up over a lady, anyway?" he said. "They're all crazy. Just think of that psychotic broad who just got sent to the insane asylum."

He was speaking of Gertrude Heitman, a housewife who was recently sentenced to an asylum for writing letters to the mayor and other government officials. A psychologist deemed that any wife interested in the inner workings of local government must be some sort of mental defective. In fact, the state legislature recently increased the number of reasons a husband could involuntarily commit his wife to an asylum, including:

- Insufficient love of pot roast

- Overly enthusiastic about geography

- Interest in maritime law

- Aversion to flamenco dancing

- Suspicion of husband's infidelity

- Inability to discern between "you're" and "your"

Morning turned into early afternoon, as Philly and I alternated between beer and whiskey. The conversation remains cloudy, although I believe he told me about his further plans for his facial recognition program, which he has taken to calling "PUSS-BOOK," mentioning that he may have found a deep-pocketed Russian investor to help finance his project.

"He said something about Woodrow Wilson running a secret child prostitution ring out of the back room of a local restaurant," said Philly. "I'm not sure I believe it, but the guy has a lot of money. So it has to at least be partially true, right?"

In my hazy state, it all made sense.

After what must have been eight drinks apiece, my young companion and I settled up with the bartender and staggered out into the warmth of the late July air. The sun was high in the sky, as it couldn't have been past one-thirty in the afternoon.

I recall squinting under the bright sun while trying to wander home the usual way. I cut through several alleyways, dodging trash cans and laundry lines. But, as I made my way toward Fourth Street, I could feel nature's call. I had not relieved myself the entire time I had been sitting with Philly, and the Poseidon in my bladder now sought revenge.

As I turned on to Fourth Street, still not entirely certain what was happening, I walked up a flight of wooden stairs and saw a bucket that looked very much like an oversized beer mug. As I faced the buildings to the east side of the street, I surmised that nobody would notice if I were to empty the contents of my bladder in this bucket. After all, my abdomen felt as if it were about to explode.

As I cast the stream from my loins, I suddenly heard the most raucous racket! I slowly began to turn around, and it quickly dawned upon me that there were roughly 1,000 people standing behind me, applauding my golden shower.

I quickly truncated the stream and jerked my drawers back to their starting position. I leaned toward the crowd beneath the stage and looked backward at the beer-shaped bucket I had found, which was emblazoned with the words "TO HELL WITH SATAN'S BREW."

"Hooray to our brother in arms!" yelled one of the matrons on the platform, who had evidently been addressing the gathering before I stumbled upon them.

"Hooray!" yelled the crowd.

It took my spirit-soaked brain more than a handful of seconds to connect what was happening. From what I could discern, there was a nearly all-female crowd cheering me as I desecrated an oversized likeness of a beer mug, not unlike the one I had had just held in my hand minutes earlier.

And then, it occurred to me – I was suddenly the unwitting guest of honor at a rally in favor of Prohibition. I had drunkenly stumbled into a demonstration organized to prevent men from drunkenly stumbling into places.

"What is your name, young man?" asked the old lady on stage with a large false bird on her hat that, frankly, had me terrified.

My mind raced.

"Shaquille," I said, thinking of a preposterous name nobody could ever have, thus leaving me untraceable.

"Well, Shaquille," she said, "I think we all agree with your position on the destructive effects of alcohol. Would you like to say a few words?" she asked.

As the applause imploring me to impart my wisdom died down, I could only hear one voice off to the left of the stage. It was a fair, familiar voice that simply said, "Oh, shit."

As I turned to look, I could see Virginia, putting her hands to her face as if she were about to witness a human birth.

Next thing I knew, I was opening my eyes and staring at a blank white ceiling. I turned my head to the right, saw a picture of President James A. Garfield on the wall, and recognized that I was in my own bedroom. I sat up, and my head began to pound like a steam engine. I realized I was still fully clothed. I looked outside and saw the sun was just beginning to set - evidently, I had slept all afternoon.

I tried to retrace my steps from earlier in the day. I recalled getting to the saloon, having discussions with Philly, walking outside, and...

OH NO.

I poured myself into my shoes, walked down to the drug store, and picked up a copy of the Milwaukee Sentinel - the city's afternoon newspaper. As I flipped to the third page, I saw a small news brief which read:

MENTAL DEFECTIVE DELIGHTS AUDIENCE OF DRYS

> Demonstrators at today's anti-liquor march were dazzled by
> the words of a former inebriate who showed the damage
> years of addiction to John Barleycorn can inflict. It is
> unknown how long the man, who demanded the audience
> call him "Shack Diesel," has been off the sauce, but he
> provided a stirring example of how alcohol can
> permanently ravage one's faculties.
>
> Mr. Diesel delighted the crowd as he urinated on a replica
> of a beer mug while complimenting several young women
> close to the stage. In a truly gracious move, he offered
> attendees "five cent moustache rides," well below the ten
> cents currently offered on the Facial Saddle futures market.
> And, he pledged to start a new organization he would call
> "Drinking is Not Awesome Except for Some of the Time
> But Usually Not and That is Something I Truly Believe and
> am Not Making Up Right This Moment"
> (DINAEFSOTTBUNATISITBAANMURTM) and offered
> any of the ladies in the front row "a position on my staff."
>
> Mr. Diesel then ran off stage without comment, leaving the
> audience cheering his bravery and commitment.

I re-read the story and then read it once again for good measure.

"I suppose that could have gone worse," I said, relieved.

As I began folding the paper up to put it away, a headline
caught my eye for a fleeting second:

"MICHIGAN POLICE BEGIN RAIDING HOMES."

August 15, 1916

Among the plethora of new things the connected age has brought us is the invention of exciting new words and phrases!

For instance, an especially voracious group of FINGER-PHONE users has adopted a new name which they wield with a pride usually displayed by Civil War veterans. Their new moniker is a sardonic twist on the word "drunk," which typically describes the socially adept party-going inebriates in American society. To show pride in their lack of social skills, this gaggle of technologically forward users has flipped the word "drunk" around and come up with the word "KNURD."

Or, as some have taken to spelling it, "NERD." (While the spelling is cleaner, this iteration of the term seems to have zero chance of ever catching on.)

Not to be outdone, a similar group has begun to flaunt their own weird credentials. A competing group of societal outcasts has taken the name from circus freak shows where entertainers eat live insects and bite the heads off of live animals. These performances, dubbed "geek" shows, are named from the German slang "geck," meaning fool, freak, or simpleton.

One wonders why these groups of undesirables didn't simply adopt the common terms for awkward outcasts, such as "dewdroppers," "waldos," or "slackers." Clearly, they have embraced their inability to speak to girls and basic lack of hygiene and attempted to empower themselves with these new terms.

But, what if this type of culture one day becomes fashionable? God help us when one day everyone who graduates from high school claims to have been a "knurd" or a "geek" during their school days! Why would anyone desire to exhibit strength by claiming weakness?

The fact that these social pariahs can now find each other has given rise to an even more troubling phenomenon: the "knurd bully."

These are the socially inept INTER-LOG users who use their technical expertise to gang up on otherwise normal people who express opinions about works of so-called "scientific fiction." For instance, user ORACLE06 enthusiastically backed the claim made by author Hugo Gernsback in his magazine series "Ralph 124C 41+" that, one day, each American would have their own device to watch moving pictures in their own homes. And, even less believably, that someday moving pictures would have SOUND!

ORACLE06's naysayers immediately pounced, pointing out that neither film nor audio can fit inside of a wire that would have to be run to every person's home to make this impossibility a reality. It would be easier to hire your own actors to come to entertain you in your own home! And likely less expensive!

For his efforts, ORACLE06 was invited to "kill yourself," "delete your account," and "light your balls on fire so you never reproduce." His home address was revealed on the INTER-LOG, and his actual identity was made known to everyone. To everyone's surprise, ORACLE06 ended up being a ten-year-old boy from Beaver Creek, Utah. Let us hope little Philo T. Farnsworth isn't too distraught to one day make something of himself!

The problem, of course, is that these roving armies of FINGER-PHONE users are often able to hide behind pseudonyms in order to attack others. As the great Oscar Wilde once said, "Give a man a mask and he will tell you the truth." Yet, in August of 1916, this witticism has evolved into, "Give a man an anonymous FINGER-PHONE account and he will lecture you about Frankenstein's origin story until you want to run your connectivity machine over with an automobile."

More importantly, let us hope the knurds and the geeks limit their attacks to one another. Hopefully, the great knurd-geek war of 1916 will settle once and for all which group reigns supreme!

Of course, connecting like-minded citizens around the country has also had political ramifications. Groups of peaceniks opposed to the United States' involvement in the War in Europe have begun forming organizations intent on demonstrating in favor of America's continued neutrality. And, unlike the protesters arrested at the Chicago preparedness parade, these anonymous FINGER-PHONE users can organize in secret outside the prying eyes of law enforcement.

Yet many anti-war protesters remain in the open. Most notable among this group is young University of Wisconsin English instructor Julia Grace Wales, who has written her own international peace plan called "Continuous Mediation Without Armistice." Her hopelessly naïve plan calls for the formation of a "Peace League" of neutral nations that she believes will help bring warring nations to the bargaining table.

Much of the anti-war sentiment has been fomented by U.S. Senator Robert M. La Follette, who claims America is being further pushed to war by powerful arms interests that have Woodrow Wilson's ear. "Fighting Bob" has called for all arms and ammunition industries to be nationalized, thinking that if the profit motive were removed, so would America's incentive to go to war.

Naturally, the anti-war demonstrations have primarily taken place on college campuses, where young men and women alike have protested outside of university buildings. One professor in the University of Wisconsin music department has written a number of anti-war songs and taken them to California, where he hopes they will spread eastward. Imagine the sight of musicians singing songs in support of stopping a war! Who has ever heard of such a thing?

Nonetheless, the giant guns are still blazing on the battlefields of France, as both sides pummel one another day after day. Despite the loss of hundreds of thousands of soldiers to this point, many FINGER-PHONE users attempt to simply make the tragedy about them.

The INTER-LOGS are full of details about users' trips to Paris or other such nonsense, posted in an attempt to make the user seem somehow connected to the war. For future reference, if you once ate a croissant in a delightful outdoor café in Marseille, it does not qualify you to comment on the barbarity of soldiers being blown apart so completely they are sent home in cigar boxes!

Further, it should not shock anyone that the FINGER-PHONE community has taken full advantage of the anti-preparedness effort. Dozens of groups with suspect names have begun cropping up, asking those with machines to "crowd fund" their attempt to stop the war in Europe. Such groups include:

- STOP THE WAR

- NO, REALLY, STOP THE WAR

- THE FUND TO STOP THE WAR

- THE STOP THE WAR FUND

- DON'T GIVE MONEY TO THE STOP THE WAR FUND, GIVE TO US

- DON'T GIVE MONEY TO "DON'T GIVE MONEY TO THE STOP THE WAR FUND, GIVE TO US," INSTEAD, GIVE TO US

And again, for some reason:

- RON PAUL FOR PRESIDENT

For a brief second, I considered sending money to "THE FUND TO STOP THE WAR" in order to pacify my love, Virginia. (Additionally, their pitch for cash was accompanied by an interesting news article telling readers "YOU WOULDN'T BELIEVE WHAT MARY TODD LINCOLN LOOKS LIKE NOW.")

But, at this point, I believe Virginia is beginning to suspect that my enthusiasm for progressive causes may not be entirely selfless. I had always considered ours to be the love that could not be spoken, only shown – and yet, it appears I have failed on both counts.

Nevertheless, I have determined I must still attempt to woo Virginia, as WillieCat has completely disappeared! I fear her absence has something to do with the story about police raids in Michigan at which I briefly glanced two weeks ago.

What were the purposes of these raids? Was law enforcement somehow made aware of the extraneous activities of wealthy investment banker Bernard Wolfe?

There may be another, more insidious, explanation. In the office last Wednesday, Basil made reference to a story he had seen that federal officers were beginning to crack down on dissent among citizens interested in politics. Evidently, thin-skinned President Wilson does not take kindly to being criticized for his ridiculous vacillations on the war issue and has sent officers out to find those engaged in what he considers "seditious" conduct.

Certainly, my discussions with Grace would fall into such a category. We both delight in shredding the weak-kneed Wilson, publicly and privately. But how could our transmissions ever be considered "unpatriotic" to the point of being criminal?

More importantly, if they are responsible for taking my true love away from me, are these federal officers aware of the damage her absence is doing to my feelings of self-worth?

Yet my romantic problems pale in comparison to some inter-couple imbroglios that have sprouted up in the news recently.

In family court, Mrs. William L. Fawcett has filed for divorce from her husband for his alleged unfaithfulness. Particularly troubling to Mrs. Fawcett is that she had to sacrifice her exalted social position in Brooklyn, New York in order to marry Mr. Fawcett, of whom her family vehemently disapproved.

Upon finding an unopened letter from Fawcett's mistress in a pair of plaid pants he wore the previous day, his wife confronted him, demanding he explain. William Fawcett denied knowing the woman who sent the letter, denied the letter was his, and denied even owning any plaid pants.

At this point, Mrs. Fawcett began reading the letter, which was from a stage actress in nearby Fond du Lac, Wisconsin.

Dear, Dear Boy:

Matinee is over and I can snatch just a little time to write to you. I have read and reread your letter many times and it makes me very happy. Also, thank you for the emblem – I am wearing it now and I cherish and value it. I shall never be without it, dear. I shall wear it always.

I must say, William L. Fawcett, of 2487 North Eighth Street, Milwaukee, Wisconsin, I live in fear that your wife will find out about our love and tear us asunder. I ask that you please not leave this letter in those plaid pants of which you are so fond, in case she finds it. If she confronts you about this letter, please do not say the letter is not yours and don't tell her you don't know who I am, as you are wont to do.

I have also enclosed a photograph of me wearing my emblem and writing this letter to you as I gaze at the photo of yourself that you gave me.

-JANE

At which point, William Fawcett said, "Wow, whoever that guy is that she wrote that letter to is probably in a lot of trouble."

In fact, romance was in the air in various newspaper stories – but not for Mr. and Mrs. William Busick of Joplin, Missouri. On the way home from the theater on Tuesday, the couple was involved in a bit of a row. When they reached their doorstep, the argument quickly escalated, and Mrs. Busick pulled a revolver from her handbag. But Mr. Busick was quicker and drew two guns before his wife could draw one, and he shot her through the heart, killing her instantly.

What a delightful couple this appeared to have been! Each one a walking armory in case some burned potatoes turned into a battle to remain above ground. It is fortunate for him that the husband actually struck his wife; the way things escalated so quickly, she no doubt had a grenade launcher in her handbag ready to eviscerate him!

But, as Otto said upon hearing the story, "We're all that couple some days, just unarmed."

Another article on the same page offers reasons why modern men are waiting longer to marry; on average, men are now waiting until the ripe age of twenty-five years to wed. As a result, the average woman must now wait until the advanced age of twenty-one to find a husband!

According to the Woman's Home Companion, the modern man "knows that it means a sentence to hard labor for him, because he knows what it costs to keep the modern family." That is why "nice, attractive but quiet girls say they can't understand why we pass them up for the flashy girl, the dance-mad girl who would doubtless make an extravagant, useless wife."

Although no one asked for her opinion, Virginia took exception to this slate of articles, asserting that women should have equal rights with men. After the laughter in the room subsided, Otto offered the scientific fact that man was made first and woman "sprang from the man."

"Quite so," said Virginia. "It is natural for the flower to come after the stem, but surely you do not call that an indication of inferiority."

One man who evidently had enough with the woman in his life was southside resident August Boguslowski, who celebrated his first wedding anniversary by trying to set his house on fire with his wife inside of it. When police officers heard the woman's cries, they entered Boguslowski's home and found the carpet saturated with kerosene and Boguslowski holding a lit match. He was fined five dollars and ordered to undergo couples counseling with the carpet.

Married men are also now in peril in the European War as England has, for the first time, begun calling on betrothed men to serve in the military. Previously, only bachelors and widowers were subject to the country's conscription act. When offered the option to either stay at home with their wives or have their limbs torn from their body in a muddy, disease-ridden field in France, one hundred percent of married men showed up for military duty.

Work was especially grueling this week, as I was given the task of typing the Sunday magazine section. Included in the features was a work of fiction called "A Prisoner of War" by a young British writer by the name of P.G. Wodehouse. Oh, how delicious is his prose! My fingers have rarely enjoyed more the experience of typing such lithe wording. If he beats the odds and becomes a writer of note, how fortunate we will all be in the long run!

In a speech on Monday, industrial commission chairman John Mitchell urged passage of both a "minimum wage" and legislation to limit work days to eight hours. Imagine! Mitchell said the shorter work day would give us the "opportunity for the cultivation of home life, the enjoyment of books, music, and wisely employed leisure."

Yet this makes little sense, as most married men would gladly give their employer back this "minimum wage" in order to avoid spending more time at home! GA!

On the night of Monday, February 21, a wireless voice signal will be sent from Rock Island, Illinois and be received in Milwaukee at the Marconi Wireless Telegraph building on the top of the Railway Exchange building. To date, these types of wireless transmissions have been limited to amateur operators and Boy Scouts. The demonstration on Monday, however, will show the commercial possibilities of wireless audio. During a recent test reception from an unknown sender, one could easily make out the word "BOOBS." What progress!

In sports news, the New York Yankees just signed John Franklin "Home Run" Baker to a contract worth $37,000 per year! The hulking five-foot-eleven, one hundred and seventy-three pound Baker was given his sobriquet after hitting an unheard of twelve home runs in 1913 with the Philadelphia Athletics. Surely, a record that will never be broken!

Baker has said the key to his massive strength is ingesting a new meal known as the ham-burger before each game. Evidently, it is beef ground, cooked, and placed on two slices of bread for ease of handling – no ham involved! While this power-packed sandwich is likely a passing fad, professional baseball has considered banning it from pre-game meals. From this point, any player receiving ham-burger in the mail will be banned for a full year!

An interesting story I typed on Wednesday followed the practice of professional baseball players changing their names, often to escape negative ethnic connotations. These aren't nicknames – in the way young Boston Red Sox pitcher George Herman Ruth goes by the moniker "Babe." Many times, players conceal their past identities completely.

For instance, Lee Magee of the St. Louis Cardinals was born Leopold Christopher Hoernschemeyer. Pirates outfielder Max "Scoops" Carey was born Maximilian Carnarius – his father was even a soldier in the German army. But, with anti-German sentiment sweeping the nation, both young German ballplayers have chosen ethnically neutral sobriquets to avoid fan anger. Feeling inspired, young Austrian catcher Abe Bortion has just changed his name to "LeBron James."

A particularly grisly story has surfaced in Des Moines, Iowa, where laborer Charles Cleveland has asked the police to help him kill his own two-month-old daughter. The baby was born without a mouth and suffers from convulsions, so Cleveland took his case to the local police to ask how he might end the child's life legally.

"Chief," Cleveland said, "won't you tell me how I can kill my baby so it won't be against the law?"

The stunned police chief forbade Cleveland from killing his daughter, instead forcing both the baby and the mother into the hospital for treatment. Within days, the child was handed over to "city mother" Mrs. M. McMichael, who will oversee an operation to save the baby's life.

The chief cited the need to protect the life of the child, no matter what stage of development it was in. As a result, the police chief immediately became the frontrunner for the 1920 Republican presidential nomination.

Health issues have also been foremost in our city, as typhoid fever is striking over thirty new people a day. It is the worst outbreak of any disease in the city since the cholera epidemic of the 1850s. At that time, Mayor Smith signed a city ordinance barring anyone from bringing diseases like cholera into the city. Not surprisingly, merely outlawing disease did nothing to stem its spread, as diseases are notoriously ignorant of municipal ordinances.

In this instance, the city has declared a "War on Typhoid." This is comforting news, as it is clear the government is deadly serious when it declares war on an amorphous phenomenon, even if that phenomenon can't be shot with a bullet. Just wait until the government someday wages a "War on Poverty!" What economic largesse will rain upon our nation!

The rumor around town is that the typhoid was the result of two dead bodies found in the city's North Avenue drinking water reservoir. Water Commissioner Ruhland adamantly put that rumor to rest, reassuring people that no dead bodies had been found in the reservoir since the sixteen found there last year.

"Whew," said the public – adding, "Wait, what?"

September 1, 1916

On Thursday, Philly and I once again enjoyed several drinks at the Oyster. And, of course, I once again regaled him with the hopelessness of my situation with Virginia.

"You just have to stand out from all the rest," he said. "She's the type of girl that has bachelors asking her on dates everywhere she goes. She's looking for something different."

I told him I was in the exact opposite predicament. "Strange women often actively seek me out in public and plead with me not to ask them out," I said, shrugging.

He kept talking without acknowledging that I was telling a joke, which concerned me. Evidently, my attempt at self-effacement was actually believable.

"You can't keep doing what you're doing," he said. "Do you know what the definition of insanity is?"

Of course I know what the definition of insanity is, so I groaned loudly. I have actually long thought that insanity is using the "insanity is doing the same thing over and over and expecting the same result" cliché over and over and expecting people not to have heard it.

"Insanity is doing the same thing over..."

"Yes, I know," I said.

"...and expecting..."

"I get it, really."

"...the same result!" he finished as if he had just said something profound enough to be carved on the Washington Monument.

"So, what do I do differently?" I said.

"I have a plan that is absolutely brilliant!" he blurted.

I knew this plan would be substandard, as I have a particular aversion to the word "brilliant." People should not be able to declare things to be "brilliant" unless they are themselves brilliant. The word grants the person making the declaration an unearned air of authority. If you are deemed brilliant by someone who gratifies themselves by filling their ears with mashed potatoes, what have you accomplished?

"Okay, let's hear it," I said, fully aware of Philly's non-brilliance. He is a man who thinks any direction he is facing is due North.

"You have to insult her," he said.

I bolted to my feet. "Cast aspersions to a woman? To make her fall in love with you? This is pure applesauce!" I said.

"Settle down and hear me out," he said.

I still had a full glass of whiskey in front of me. So in all honesty, my threat to walk out was an empty one all along.

"It works though," he said. "It's crazy when you think about it."

"It was crazy long before I thought about it," I snapped back. Who can resist metaphysical humor?

"Think about it. She has suitors surrounding her everywhere, all the time," he said. "She clearly wants a man who challenges her and doesn't accede to her every demand."

In my pants pocket, I could feel the poem I had written to her earlier in the day that compared my love for her to a field of begonias.

"But demonstrating your masculine independence is quite different than hurling insults," I said.

"It's called 'negging,'" he said. "You offer a backhanded compliment to a woman to catch her off guard and reduce her confidence. At that point, you have her attention. She will then be more affectionate to try to win back your approval."

"Where did you hear this nonsense?" I said.

"It's all science," he said. "It's been proven over centuries. No woman in history has liked feeling like she's just like everyone else."

"Shouldn't science first be working on a cure for smallpox?" I said.

When I returned home, I began writing out some acrid zingers that were sure to make Virginia fall for me. I tossed out my passionate love poem and instead penned a number of risible gibes to raise her dander.

On Friday morning, I strolled into the office with my chest out, projecting strength and independence. As I calmly sat in my seat, I slowly removed the folded piece of paper containing my withering calumnies and set it to the right of my workstation. From the corner of my right eye, I could see Philly settle in behind the staircase to get a better look at my impending demonstration of manliness.

"How are you today?"

From my left side, I heard the unmistakable voice of my Virginia, fully unaware of the aural lashing she was about to receive. I turned, looked at her, and immediately felt my stomach contract as if I had been starving for a month. She smiled, and she was as beautiful as ever, with eyes that could alone power a small city. As I looked at her unblemished visage, I could feel sweat begin to trickle down the back of my shirt.

But I immediately remembered that her comeliness was the reason I needed to confront her and set myself apart from the rest of the other nobodies competing for her affections.

I quickly glanced at my list, gulped, and began.

"Virginia," I said, "were you aware that you smell strongly of boiled cabbage?"

She squinted, sat back in her chair, and took a deep breath.

"I'm sorry, but the 'Eau de Boiled Cabbage' perfume was half-off at the department store last week," she said, smiling.

This was not how this was supposed to go. I looked at the next item on my list.

"Virginia," I said, "were you aware that you resembled a porcupine with an overdue library book?"

"Are you aware you resemble a man who has never seen a naked woman in person?" she shot back.

I could hear Philly trying to control his laughter from fifteen feet away. He was clearly holding his mouth and snorting through his nose. I shuffled uncomfortably in my seat. The porcupine line had taken me an hour to write.

"Virginia," I said, "are you aware that you are too poor to pay attention?"

With this line, she chuckled boisterously.

"Did you two morons actually cook up this plan to 'neg' me?" she said.

It was clear she was referring to both me and Philly, who at this point was doubled over in laughter. "You think women don't know this strategy?" she said. "This may be the most pathetic attempt at courtship that the world has ever seen."

Clearly, my cover had been blown! I grabbed my sixteen-page list of insults and ran from the room, sprinting up the stairs while cursing modern science for making a fool of me. When will science progress to the point where two teenage boys can simply make the perfect woman in their own bedroom, then inexplicably turn into the most popular kids in their school when a prosthetic woman helps them throw a party at their parents' home? What would possibly be weird about that?

My combination of discomfort with both women and science was perhaps outdone this week by Professor Robert Grimshaw of New York University, who gave a speech in town in which he listed fifty-seven ways Americans are less efficient than Germans. Grimshaw has spent twenty years researching German efficiency and claims women are the source of every one of America's efficiency lapses. "Men are what women make them," Grimshaw told an audience this week.

At the end of Grimshaw's speech, a lady reporter asked him whether he considered it particularly efficient to spend twenty years compiling an arcane list of fifty-seven inefficiencies, only to discuss them in front of a room of twenty people.

Grimshaw paused momentarily, and then said, "Oh, shit."

Women are also to blame for the decline of musical comedy, according to Seymour Rice, manager of the Grand Opera house. Rice said he believes short dresses worn on the street now replicate those previously only worn on stage, and men can see everything they want outside the theater.

"With this parade that you can see on any street any day of the week – and with a variety of shapes, and colors – with the women properly equipped in all departments, why should folk pay their way into a theater to see the same thing and fewer of them?" Rice complained.

In order to draw more men to the theater, Rice said he was going to feature more male fantasy pieces that show women doing things men would never see outside the stage. For instance, one upcoming play is said to feature a woman using foul language! No longer will the theater feature family-friendly fare like the hit play about the pleasures of smoking, "Get that Fag in My Mouth!"

Two days ago, I typed up the strangest of letters to the editor. Entitled "A MANLY CONFESSION," it was written by an anonymous penman who indicated his desire to dress as a woman.

"I should revel in velvets, in silks, and satins, in plumes and ruffles, in rich or delicate colors, in daring and dashing modes, in endless variety suited to my whim, to the weather or to the occasion," the writer said. "It would be an artistic gratification. But I don't dare."

This gentleman pointed out that, in the days of knighthood, men were truly brave and out-dressed the women. Yet in modern days, the only extravagance a man is allowed is the occasional cravat. He asserted that men are secretly "slaves to fashion," a state from which modern men are "too cowardly to free ourselves."

Surely this was another trick being played on me by young Philly! A man desiring to dress as a woman? I suppose he would want to be called a woman's name, too! One would think if he were to show up to vote wearing a dress, he wouldn't be allowed to cast a ballot, which would be best for all of us. If he were allowed to choose our politicians and influence our laws, it would be mere years before it was considered good for a man's public image to declare himself a lady! What's next, are we going to find out that a leader of a national black rights association is actually a white person?

On Thursday, a patron walked into a local tavern and asked for a drink but said he didn't have enough money. So, Charlie Ross offered to trade a Bible for a glass of whisky. The outraged bartender immediately called the police and had the man arrested and ordered out of town. As it turns out, the Bible was stolen from a city mission.

"Using the Bible as currency is desecrating our most sacred work," said the bartender, who has evidently read all six pages of the Bible that don't reference either forgiveness or compassion.

This week, the federal government also told women and young girls they would no longer be allowed to collect their mail via general delivery, rather than having it delivered to their homes. Under the current law, a reason must be given to collect mail at the post office, and workers said they have heard every excuse possible, from "I don't want the landlady to read my mail," to "my mother and father are divorced and I don't want my father to read the letters my mother sends me," to "for business reasons."

Uncle Sam suspects many of these reasons are simply given so women can carry out illicit affairs with men to whom they are not married or for young girls to receive mail from older men. One postal worker recounted the time a husband and wife unknowingly ran into each other at the post office both picking up general mail! Unable to find anything in his pockets, the poor husband had to remove his hat and pretend as if he was mailing it to his cousin in Illinois. Unfortunately, he didn't even know the address, so some lucky citizen of a small Illinois town just received a free hat!

This, it would seem, would be part of the allure of the FINGER-PHONE. Since letters are delivered in private without the post office, it seems the machine could easily facilitate the activities of philandering husbands and wives. Let us pray this is not what the future holds, as nine percent of all marriages already end in divorce. Imagine the social catastrophe that awaits if that number were to double!

September 15, 1916

How the world is changing!

On Friday, a young gentleman named Rudolph Weinkopf was found dead at his job as a hotel porter. Yet, when an autopsy was conducted, it was found out that young Rudolph was actually a woman! This confounded poor Rudolph's fellow hotel employees, who had spent many nights in fraternal bond with the young "lad."

The deceased had even been known to take a cocktail and smoke a cigarette, and one colleague even said he once saw Rudolph read Dostoevsky! In retrospect, his chums noted that young Rudolph had been avoiding women, but they thought it was because the boy was fourteen years old! Given the shame felt by the hotel, it seems likely that this type of storyline will never be revived again in any type of popular entertainment.

On Tuesday, a man was fined five dollars for operating a motor vehicle while intoxicated! When the officer pulled Gerhardt Steimke over, he performed the typical drunk driving test – the suspected inebriate is forced to breathe into a mason jar containing a young frog. If the frog begins writing letters to ex-lovers, the driver's breath is clearly tainted with alcohol and he is arrested. The contents of the jar are then sent by train to a testing laboratory in New York City, and, while the alleged perpetrator waits in prison, the final results are rendered in a short eight months.

This is a true head-scratcher, as anyone who can afford an automobile should also be able to pay someone to drive them around in it after sampling too much of the grape and grain. In addition, driving after imbibing alcohol is illegal! Once word gets out of the newly passed law, surely no one will again play this game of chance with his life. Several years ago, one city resident was arrested for riding a horse while intoxicated. Only it was the horse who was besotted – after eating a bushel of fermented apples – and washing those apples down with four Tom Collinses!

Recently, the Post has been providing more practical news to its readers, in order to improve their everyday lives. On Thursday, I was tasked with typing out a news piece advising readers on how to gain those extra pounds they just can't seem to pack on. A new wonder drug known as Sargol will allegedly "coax the stomach and intestines to literally soak up the fattening elements of your blood," where your starving cells will be fed with delicious fat.

Soon, "your cheeks will fill out and those hollows about your head, neck and bust will disappear." It is finally about time someone tackled the emaciation epidemic in America. Imagine one hundred years from now when mere skeletons will roam the national landscape!

This was only the second most important scientific breakthrough of the week, behind Dr. Arthur Reynolds' article in The American Magazine, in which he determined that the wearing of hats is the sole reason men go bald on their heads.

"When a man wears a hat, it applies pressure on the entire vascular supply of the scalp," said the doctor.

Contradicting Dr. Reynolds' theory is Miss Dorothy Osborn of Ohio State University, who claims a one hundred percent probability that a man or woman will be bald if he or she has two bald parents.

You may be asking yourself, "Where are all these bald women to which Mrs. Osborn is referring?" She says that, according to the American Genetic Association, bald women are more prevalent than we think, "because women can conceal baldness much more easily than can men."

Imagine the anger of a husband who had a bald daughter, only to find out after the fact that his wife was, in fact, secretly bald all along! To what lengths will women go to hide their true looks from men? Imagine a day when women's hair color, eye color, height, and bodily proportions are all selected from a menu. Surely men will have grounds for a class-action lawsuit alleging fraud!

Yesterday, Alexander Johnson, chairman of the National Council on the Prevention of Feeblemindedness, gave a speech in which he urged segregating over 400,000 of society's criminals and feebleminded unfortunates into a separate geographic area. Johnson claimed more than one-fourth of all prostitutes are feebleminded and sending them away could rid society of the ills they cause.

Asked what this new land composed of feebleminded criminals, prostitutes, and single mothers would be called, Johnson answered, "Florida."

On Friday, George Romas was arrested on a white slavery charge for forcing seventeen-year-old Stella Romas into marrying him. George Romas had taken Stella to Louisiana, telling her he had a job for her in his cousin's candy store. When they arrived, he showed her a telegram he said was from state authorities which threatened to arrest her if she did not marry him. After the marriage, she tried to escape but was assaulted and detained by Romas and another man.

While Romas' sentence is yet unknown, the maximum charge for "white slavery" is five years in prison and a $10,000 fine. For "black slavery?" A two dollar fine and mandatory mumbled apology.

It certainly seems as though women are making progress in both society and politics. Last week, a group of suffragist leaders tore into President Wilson for allowing Congress to adjourn without taking up a constitutional amendment allowing for nationwide suffrage. Ms. Alice Paul, chairman of the Congressional Union for Women declared, "It is action, not words, which will appeal to suffragists."

It appears Wilson is satisfying fewer women than I am these days!

Yet, according to some, politics won't even be necessary in the near future. Last week, Harry Phillips, the former mayor of East London, came to America and declared that our country would be a "utopia" by 1966 because of its "progressive methods." Mr. Phillips predicted that, in fifty years, America would have no saloons, full employment, and labor would be working harmoniously with its bosses.

Further, Phillips said that America's progressivism would soon root out the "evil influence" of liquor. On this last point, one can only hope Captain Phillips' boat was overtaken by pirates on the return trip to England. This may seem mean-spirited, but what a story it would make for the moving pictures!

In fact, that same day, a story appeared on Philly's table about a man whose wife was distressed because he demanded to have a beer every night with dinner and demanded to be able to smoke cigarettes in the house. In order to pacify this woman, the man went outside to enjoy his tobacco, but he was often called queer names by passersby, so he moved into the barn behind his house to shield himself from the insults. Then, one night while lighting his cigarette, the barn went up in flames, burning him alive! And thus, the lesson - not being able to smoke is killing people!

This is just more evidence of the insidious nannyist philosophy that has recently become pervasive. In a speech last week to the Chicago Normal College, University of Wisconsin professor of psychology Dr. Michael Vincent O'Shea counseled parents to cease scolding young boys for having dirty hands and poor table manners! Imagine! Yet O'Shea also counseled against allowing young people to do the new dances of the time, instead urging them to stick to the dances that develop chivalry, and suggested that a boy of sixteen or seventeen should not be allowed to show interest in a young woman. O'Shea argued that a man should be at least twice that age before wooing a girl of sixteen or seventeen!

The only children for whom I have any sympathy are those who have recently been stricken with whooping cough, which has become an epidemic around America. Thousands of children have been made to wear colored armbands with the words "Whooping Cough" on them to warn passersby of the danger of contagion. These young Hester Prynnes have been forced to wear the Scarlet Letter of disease, making them pariahs in their formative years!

Imagine if adults were made to wear armbands in public listing all of the diseases with which they were afflicted! This would almost certainly be a violation of privacy. Although, I would certainly support requiring women to make an armband disclosure as to whether they were bald.

As for personal matters, I received quite a scare today. When I got home from the Oyster, my telephone began ringing. I rushed to pick up the receiver and heard only heavy breathing on the line.

"Who is this?" I demanded to know.

"GET OUT!" yelled a female voice on the other line.

"Excuse me?" I asked.

"Take your INTER-LOG machine," she said. "They are coming!"

The line clicked dead and, before I could hang up the receiver, I could see police sirens flickering outside the window of my apartment.

"Search every one!" I heard, as I poked my head out of the window and saw four police officers, papers in hand, entering the ground floor of my building.

I don't normally take the word of anonymous callers terribly seriously, but this confluence of coincidences suggested I immediately do so. I ran to the corner of my living room, grabbed my stack of FINGER-PHONE papers, and quickly shoved them into a hole in my bedroom closet wall that had been chewed open by rats. I unplugged my INTER-LOG device from the phone cord and walked it over to the window, placing it delicately on the window sill.

I swung both legs out of the window, landing both feet solidly on the ledge outside. I took the FINGER-PHONE, lifted it, and was able to shove it on to the roof of the apartment building. I then pulled myself up to the roof, just as I heard the officers enter my home from the front door.

"It's gotta be here somewhere," said one officer.

"The papers from the Michigan broad's house say he lived around here," another lower-voiced policeman said.

"Clearly, this guy lives alone," said the first cop. "No woman would live in a place like this."

What would the world think if they knew some policemen had such shabby manners?

"We'd know exactly where this treasonous dirtbag lived if those incompetent dolts in Michigan hadn't let her escape," said the first officer.

"Well, if we can't find this guy even with the few pages they were able to find from her house, they'll be saying the same thing about us," said low-voice.

I heard footsteps as they shuffled through my house. As I heard officer number one rummage through my closet, I heard him yell, "Is this a Tudor collar?"

Low-voice began laughing. "It would take a diseased mind to wear that in public," he said. "He's clearly not right in the 'ol noggin. Maybe we've found our guy."

"I don't see anything else here," said the first cop, after several minutes of crashing and banging. I breathed a sigh of relief. Clearly, he must be under five-foot-seven, as he couldn't have been one of their better officers!

"On to the next one," said low-voice.

"This poor guy," said officer shorty drawers.

I heard the door close behind them and poked my head down to confirm the coast was clear. I swung down to the ledge, grabbed the FINGER-PHONE, and bounded back in through the window.

It was immediately clear to me how I had become a target of law enforcement. My dear Grace escaped when officers invaded her home, and she had only left a select few pages behind. This left my identity a mystery to the police. Had they obtained her full archive of our correspondence, they would have been able to pinpoint me easily. I have kept the list of those who can view my musings to a fairly limited community of INTER-LOG enthusiasts (if you are reading this, you are one of them, and YOU ARE WELCOME). So there is no way police could find my information by pretending to be someone they weren't. Who has ever heard of a cop adopting a false persona to investigate a crime?

(As an ancillary note, my disappointment at learning for certain that her home had been raided in large part because of discussions she had with me was more than offset by the joy I felt that she had actually kept all our communications to one another! My conscience burns, but my heart sings!)

Perhaps the most nagging unanswered question is just what exactly WillieCat and I had done wrong. And who wants our conversations silenced?

Clearly, President Woodrow Wilson has an interest is suppressing dissent, and my lengthy disquisitions about our flaccid commander-in-chief would certainly qualify as political criticism.

In his past, Wilson has shown a predilection for using the state to quash dissent, and he may see this new technology as a threat. Citizens speaking up in earlier times typically had to do so through third parties if they wanted their voices to be heard by a widespread audience. But with the FINGER-PHONE, unregulated speech by common citizens can be dispersed to many people without the filter of a newspaper editor or a printing press for pamphlets.

One competing theory being floated on the INTER-LOGS is that, ultimately, it will be newspapers themselves who lead a crackdown on the unabated sharing of information. If citizens are able to discuss news stories and share information without the aid of a daily paper, the great press empires of America could be neutered as their revenues shriveled.

But how could newspapers start arresting regular citizens? The link is quite simple! Reporters and police officers often work very closely; their jobs are frequently dependent on one another. Newspapers sharing information with law enforcement, and vice-versa, can aid in catching criminals. In doing so, favors are often exchanged. A paper may overlook misdeeds by certain officers if given exclusive information on meatier stories of more public interest.

It would, then, be in the police department's best interest to keep this symbiotic relationship afloat. If the millionaire press moguls could offer favors to the police to keep a vigorous status quo, they most certainly would.

Thus, the irony reveals itself! What if I am being hunted by my own newspaper? What if I am contributing to the demise of an industry that currently provides my paychecks? More importantly, what if a reporter at our paper catches wind of my activity? I could be felled by the printed word! (As I frequently say, whoever says the pen is mightier than the sword hasn't been stabbed by either one.)

But, there is a more pressing question monopolizing my mind. Where is WillieCat?

October 1, 1916

Two weeks later and the mystery of my dear Grace's whereabouts is still unsolved.

Even though I have not received another unannounced visit from the boys in blue, I have been on high alert for spies that may be tracking my whereabouts. I have been walking home from work in unfamiliar patterns, just to keep my would-be capturers at bay. On Thursday, I crawled home on all-fours just to evade detection and avoid any suspicion!

On Friday, my new path home took me by the XX Saloon - a tavern I typically try to avoid, as it is infested with society's most down-and-out inebriates. As I turned the corner to Wells Avenue and saw the door to the saloon, I couldn't believe my eyes. There was the villainous Bertrand Nehls, Virginia's lover!

This incantation of Bertrand was very different, however. His tie was half undone, his thick black hair looked as if it hadn't been combed in a week, and there appeared to be a yellow sauce of some kind caked on his lapels.

As he looked toward me, his eyes appeared to be coated in glass, and it took him several breaths to realize it was me. Suddenly, his face twisted into one of anger and vengeance, and he began running toward me.

Upon weighing my options for a millisecond, I decided the best option was to flee. Clearly, Bertrand had some internal issues to work out and my face was set to be his therapist.

I turned and ran as fast as I could. I took a left turn on Wells Street, then a right turn on Third Street, then another left turn on Mason Street. As I turned to see if he followed me, I felt an arm around my neck from behind – he had anticipated my route and cut me off at the pass!

Bertrand threw me to the ground, but I grabbed his jacket and brought him to the street with me. We rolled around on the tobacco spit-soaked pavement, neither of us able to free our arms enough to land a solid punch on the other.

"What are you doing?" I yelled at him, after a brief moment when I could catch my breath. "Are you drunk?" I asked him, rhetorically. Upon being so close to him, I could tell he had been possessed by John Barleycorn.

He rolled over to his side and sat upright.

"You ruined my life," he said. "You couldn't leave Virginia alone, could you?"

I was puzzled and perplexed. I was perpuzzled.

"I did no such thing!" I responded. "You're the one who ended up with her! Shouldn't I be the one chasing you down and raining blows on your skull?"

"She's gone," he said. "Left me last week. I've been drinking ever since," he slurred.

"That's got nothing to do with me," I said.

"It has everything to do with you," he answered. "Even though she was with me, every night it was 'did you hear what Sebastian did today,' or 'you wouldn't believe how Sebastian tried to win me over this morning.' Even though she was my girl, your attempts to romance her made my relationship efforts look inadequate."

"That is terrible," I said. That is great, I thought.

"I made myself look like a fool on a daily basis," I told him. "You never really had anything to worry about."

"You never even really loved her," he said. "You're much better suited for this comely married woman in Michigan," he added.

I shot to my feet. "WHAT?" I barked.

"You gotta be more careful who you share personal information with," he said. "You never know who could be reading it."

"You...you...have a device?" I said.

"I'm rich, stupid," he answered. "Of course I have a FINGER-PHONE. And I've read all of your posts."

"Wait. Did you show them to Virginia?" I asked.

"No, of course not," he said. "Even though you ruined my life, some of them are pretty funny. And if you were failing spectacularly with Virginia, why would I show her something that would make you more endearing?"

He said he began following me early in the year under a nom de plume and we had jibed one another back and forth several times.

"I wrote you a message back in January about President Roosevelt," he said. "Got you really worked up."

"You're BOOTYCRUSHR?" I said.

"Yep."

"Huh."

As I recall, in addition to our acrid exchanges, BOOTYCRUSHR had set up an INTER-LOG where he provides daily "recaps" of episodes of serialized entertainment. At first, he started writing a six-hundred word explanation for each comic strip that appeared in the newspaper, including giving away all the jokes contained therein. Then, he began writing summaries of all the serialized fictional magazine articles that appeared in the Sunday paper every week and provided each with a letter grade.

This seemed like a fairly flawed business model to begin with. It all hinged on someone of preternatural talent spending months or years creating a unique piece of art or literature then gifting it to the world. Then, a less talented FINGER-PHONE user would take that art, describe it, and try to earn INTER-LOG views just by virtue of associating himself with its genius. Clearly, commenting on culture is not the same as creating culture – the former are simply mollusks feeding off the latter. (It got completely out of hand when he began recapping articles written by other recappers.)

"I actually have some good news for you," he said.

"And what's that?"

"You get the chance to help me win her back," he said.

"Why wouldn't I just try to win her for myself?"

"Because she left me for some other man," he said. "Some upstanding member of high society."

"And why would I help you wrest her from this other man's clutches?"

"If you don't, I'll tell her all about your little married criminal girlfriend," he said. "And I think the police would be interested in knowing where you live," he added.

He was blackmailing me into helping him get back together with the woman I loved. He was as dastardly as I thought all along! (And now that I remember I have read his writings, I know he isn't aware of the difference between "its" and "it's." His disdain for me is second only to his contempt for elementary school grammar!)

I had no choice but to help. Living a life without Virginia in my arms was preferable to living my life in the arms of the prison system.

"I couldn't get her to want me. How am I supposed to talk her into once again wanting you?" I asked.

"I have a plan all figured out," he said. "I know a place they are going to be together on Wednesday night. It is a society fundraiser for Charles Evans Hughes, and the nominee himself will be there. All we need to do is slip some pills into the drink of this new beau of hers, and, when he begins acting erratically, we will be there to save her."

"Into her new beau's drink," I said.

"What?"

"You're using the passive voice," I said. "It is unbecoming."

"Do you want me to punch you again?"

"I would prefer that you do not."

"It is an airtight plan – my superior intellect has figured out every angle," he said. "I'll be at your house at six o'clock on Wednesday night. Wear your nicest formal wear. If you botch this, you'll be wearing stripes."

As I bid the scheming Bertrand goodbye, I immediately began to dread this new plan to extricate Virginia from the clutches of a lover who, in all honesty, was likely a better catch than either of us. I contemplated whether I could secretly alter the plan to make Bertrand seem like the fool, thereby making myself the hero. But, if I were to stray from his initial plan, he could always give her the damaging information about me. It would be a murder-suicide. (I also remembered to block BOOTYCRUSHR as soon as I got home.)

At work on Monday, I remained silent while working next to Virginia. I dutifully typed the story of Mr. John Schedler of New York, who had come to our bustling city to make a living counterfeiting large treasury bills. Evidently, Schedler thought he could take advantage of the trusting Midwesterners who rarely questioned his phony bills.

At first, Schedler would take a five-dollar note, paint over the Roman numeral "V" and instead insert the number "10." Finding that too labor intensive, Schedler would then simply draw the number "10" on a piece of paper and hand it to a cashier. As time went on,

Schedler scrapped even that plan and began just handing random objects to a store clerk, saying "Here is a ten-dollar bill, trust me." Schedler was caught when one store clerk noticed that the bill he had been handed featured the portrait of not Andrew Jackson, but Grover Cleveland. Also, it was drawn on a salami sandwich.

In St. Louis, John Kearne and his wife were touring Shaw's botanical gardens when Kearne asked the gardener about a specific flower. The gardener told Kearne the flower was called "dumbcane," as it renders one speechless if it touches his tongue.

Kearne, who believed his wife was too talkative, walked over to her and asked her to close her eyes and open her mouth. When she obeyed, he put the flower in her mouth. A day later, while resting in the city hospital, Mrs. Kearne regained her speech and John Kearne was forced to pay for the overnight medical care. "I didn't have faith in what that gardener said, but sometimes my wife talks too much, and I thought I'd try it," said Kearne to the newspaper. Fortunately for Kearne, now he knows what literally every conversation with his wife will be about for the remainder of their marriage.

But Kearne's mental acuity far surpasses that of local man Arthur W. Seyferlich, who yesterday filed to have his marriage annulled. Seyferlich, who was married in April of this year, said he only submitted his paperwork this week because he had forgotten he was married!

He said it was his wife, Mary, that obtained the marriage certificate and made all the wedding plans back in April, but he has no recollection of any aspect of his wedding day. His wife left him shortly after the ceremony, so he claims he had completely forgotten that he was, in fact, still betrothed.

One man who likely wishes he never married is local division manager Jacob Jonas, who noticed something puzzling about his wife, Marie. Jonas worried about the fact that, when he and Marie had dinner, she never had an appetite, and he did everything he could to ensure she didn't starve to death. He suggested diets, doctors, and even offered to take her on a trip to the country to restore her taste for food.

But Jonas also noticed that, although she never ate, Marie kept gaining weight. When she reached a suspicious level of plump, he searched the house and found a pile of candy boxes in the backyard bearing the label of the "Rueckheim Bros. & Eckstein Candy Company."

It turns out the manager of the candy company was chocolatier Julius A. Hafner, whose autographed photo Jonas had found with the boxes of chocolate. One day, Jonas followed Marie to the municipal pier, where she boarded a steamship destined for Charlevoix, Michigan. Jonas then took a train to Michigan, where he confronted his wife and her candy supplier, demanding a divorce on the spot.

While it is easy to feel bad for Jonas, imagine an America where chubby women are no longer revered. If, one day, large women are treated with suspicion and not as our queens, make sure to blame Mrs. Marie Jonas!

Fortunately, the week did feature one hero. On Monday, laborer Thomas Mullen and his colleague Joseph Kournske were riding their horse-drawn carriage through the city, but the horse, feeling the load was too heavy, began laboring. Kournske jumped down from the wagon and began beating the horse until it groaned in pain.

A man in an automobile saw what was happening and quickly sped to the home of nearby female police officer Alice Clemente. "There's a couple of teamsters trying to massacre a poor old horse down on Kilbourn Street," he told the officer, who leaped in the car before even putting her uniform on.

When she approached Kournske, she said, "I'm a police officer. Quit beating that horse."

"I don't believe it," he snorted. "And if you come near here, I'll beat the stuffin' out of you."

When he turned around to see Clemente, he was looking directly into the barrel of her revolver. She then cracked him in the face with her gun and landed a half-dozen blows with her fists. Then, the five-foot-five officer dragged him into the waiting automobile while on-duty officers showed up.

"Gee," said Kournske as he and Mullen were taken to prison. "That dame packs an awful kick in her left."

Little did Clemente know the horse was wanted on three counts of homicide!

On Wednesday night, Bertrand showed up at my front door ten minutes late. He had bandages wrapped around his hand.

"Are you injured?" I said.

He said he was not. He explained that, at fundraisers held by members of high society, rich patrons had taken to expressing solidarity with the French and English soldiers in Europe by wearing head bandages.

"You know what the Allied soldiers could use?" I said.

"American troops to help crush the Central Powers."

"Of course it's an empty gesture," he said. "It makes rich people feel like they're doing something. You could take all the actual difference these people make and fit it in a thimble. They're just doing it to prove to themselves that they care more than everyone else."

"I presume the more bandage on your head you wear, the more in tune you are with the common soldier stuck in the mud in the Somme?" I said.

"Yes. And given that we have to mask our identities, we are going to care more than every rich hog's anus there," he answered.

"Be careful," I said. "You're starting to sound like a Wilson voter."

We began to wrap the bandages around our heads.

"Here's how it will work," he said. "I know my father's lawyer, Benson Thatcher, is on the list, along with his butler. But, I also happen to know that Thatcher will not be attending this evening's fundraiser, as he had to be in Sheboygan on a business matter this evening."

He explained that he and I, under the cover of head wound wraps, would play the roles of Benson Thatcher and his butler. Once inside, we would split apart to find Virginia and the new lover she had taken. Every effort would then be made to pour a powder provided by Bertrand into this gentleman's drink, rendering him incapable of controlling himself.

"It's foolproof," I said.

"You're damned right," he shot back. "We had better get to the Pfister Hotel. Hughes is just finishing up a whistle-stop speech to fifty thousand people down at the rail yards. We have to do this before he gets to the high-dollar event," he said.

We set off for the hotel looking like tuxedo-wearing mummies. My tuxedo was actually gifted to me from my father, so it hung loosely around my arms and waist area.

"Can I ask you a question?" I said, already granting myself one.

"Sure," said Bertrand.

"Don't you think it's quite a coincidence that you and I – two men with FINGER-PHONES – both just happened to fall for the same woman?"

"It would seem against the odds, yes," he answered.

"How exactly did you meet Virginia, again?" I asked, boldly seizing a third question.

"Honestly, I only met her because of your blog," he said.

"What?"

"Yeah, you mentioned that there was a beautiful young woman who was gainfully employed in your office, and I decided to wait outside the newspaper for her one day."

"You staked her out?"

"I wouldn't put it that way. I simply accidentally bumped into her – except for the 'accidentally' part."

I was done asking questions. Knowing I played a role in his

meeting Virginia, thus setting the stage for my own demise, was too much to handle. Bertrand kept talking about his plan to pen a series of children's books about a young wizard attending an English boarding school, but I tried to ignore his fanciful nonsense.

We entered the Pfister's brass doors and made our way up the stairs toward the ballroom. What an ornate hotel - certainly fit for a presidential candidate! It will no doubt delight visitors for the next century and beyond.

I was having trouble seeing out of my bandages, but Bertrand was still talking, so I followed the sound of his voice. He was going on about his new INTER-LOG idea, called "Things Caucasians Typically Enjoy." As we made our way to the check-in table, I heard him say, "Benson Thatcher, here, with my trusty butler Mauricio."

"Ah, yes, Mr. Thatcher, please make your way in. And if I do say, bless you for your support for the wounded troops."

Surprisingly, our entrance into the ballroom went as smoothly as a gravy sandwich. As I pulled the bandages away from my eyes, I was able to look at the ornate room, decorated with every accouterment befitting a major party candidate.

In the middle of the crowd of about a hundred people, there was a record player dishing out the hits everyone wanted to hear played. I had heard of high-society "Edison concerts" like this, where wealthy people gather to listen to music on the phonograph. As I surveyed, the Victrola was playing Carl Reubens' controversial hit, "Lover, I Would Like to Put my Moustache on You."

"I like a lot of his older stuff better," I told Bertrand.

"Shut it," he barked. "We are not here to socialize."

Just then, I saw her incandescent visage. Virginia was standing with a man about my height, who was also wearing a heavy bandage on his head. She, conversely, was wearing a single-wrap variety that screamed "concerned, yet subtle."

I poked Bertrand and pointed. "Jackpot!" he yelled.

We slowly walked the fifty feet toward the couple, my stomach feeling unwell. I wasn't sure if I was going to be able to speak – it was as if I had "dumbcane" placed in my mouth.

Before I knew it, we were upon the couple. Bertrand took Virginia's hand, kissed it, and bowed.

"Benson Thatcher," he said, shaking the mystery guest's hand.

"Hello, Mr. Thatcher," said Virginia. "Weren't you supposed to be in Sheboygan this evening?"

"Uh, no," said the fake Benson Thatcher. "The client I was to visit was sadly bitten by a moose and could not meet."

We looked at each other. He shrugged.

"Well, I'm very glad you made it, even if it took a hungry moose tragedy to make it happen," she said.

"Please, let me introduce you to Duke Rudolf von Biarnex of Norway."

I could have sworn I had heard that name recently. Was he in the news? Had he brought news of the war? And how did

Virginia end up with royalty?

"This is my butler, Mauricio," said Bertrand. "He is from Peru," he added.

This appeared to be an improvisation on his part. At no point did he mention my character would be from a foreign land, and I had no clue how a Peruvian accent landed on the ear!

"Yes, hello, ma'am," I said curtly.

"Certainly the Duke must be thirsty," said Bertrand. "I insist on purchasing him a drink. Please come with me."

He took the Duke and led him toward the bar, leaving Mauricio alone with Virginia.

"Please, tell me all about yourself. What was your name, again?" she said.

I wasn't quite sure I remembered. "My name is Montalban, ma'am," I said in a high-pitched voice.

"Are you sure?"

"Quite sure, ma'am."

"That is certainly an interesting accent you have there, Montalban," she said. This was not going well – rich people aren't supposed to talk to the lowly servants!

"Yes, ma'am."

"It kind of sounds more Italian than Peruvian, if I must say so. But you've probably lived all over. Oh, how I wish I could travel."

"Yes, ma'am."

"That is quite the tribute to the troops you're wearing on your head there. You must truly feel the pain of the soldiers fighting in Europe."

"Yes, ma'am. And yours is delightful, too, ma'am."

"Well, I'm firmly against the United States becoming entangled in that blasted war, but I do feel for the brave young men fighting to save their home countries," she said.

"Maybe you can wear it in honor of the wounded hearts you have caused men all over this nation," I said.

She glared at me. "Excuse me?" she said loudly.

"Hey, we're back," said Bertrand, pulling the Duke by the arm, glasses of champagne in their hands. "Oh, look – the justice is here!"

Indeed, during my brief encounter with Virginia, Justice Charles Evans Hughes had entered the room to great applause. As Bertrand and the Duke sipped on their half-empty drinks, Hughes began to speak.

"I come here representing a reunited Republican Party, ready for victory and service," Hughes began.

"Boooooo!" yelled Duke Rudolf von Biarnex of Norway, whose balance appeared to be compromised.

The cavernous room went silent. I looked at Bertrand, who locked eyes with me. Clearly, his magic powder was taking effect. He nodded in approval.

Hughes, who had given three major speeches in the past two days, continued unabated.

"It was under Republican auspices that those policies were adopted that will make possible the development of the United States, for we are all sharers in the prosperity of America-"

"I CORDIALLY INVITE YOU TO GO HAVE INTERCOURSE WITH YOURSELF!" yelled the Duke, curiously devoid of any sort of Norwegian accent.

"Wait!" I thought. Was I hallucinating? This couldn't be!

I leaned over and grasped the Duke's head wrap and gave it a firm tug. As it unraveled, I began to recognize just who this member of Norwegian "royalty" was.

I saw the face of my college chum Boomer Mills!

"Boomer!" I yelled.

"Who?" Virginia asked.

Unable to stand, Boomer grabbed my head and pulled me to the floor, unraveling my bandage in the process.

Virginia gasped. "Sebastian?"

"I can explain!"

As I tried to break free from Boomer's grasp, I could see Bertrand begin to shuffle backward slowly, in order to extricate himself from this scene.

Virginia glared at him.

"Don't tell me..." she said.

"It was his idea!" he yelled, pointing at me as I tried to perform a Duke-ectomy from my person. "He has a secret girlfriend who's on the run from the law and he talks to her with this futuristic typewriter!" he screamed.

"And he only met you because I was talking about you on my electronic communication machine!" I gasped, nearly out of breath. It was far less effective a condemnation of Bertrand than I had hoped.

"I CORDIALLY INVITE YOU TO GO HAVE INTERCOURSE WITH YOURSELF" screamed Boomer.

"All of you morons, leave at once!" barked Virginia, pointing toward the door. Soon, security officers were upon all three of us, dragging us backward through the hall toward the door.

It was during this brief interlude that I fully grasped Boomer's plan. He had me place the advertisement in the newspaper not to help a friend, but to fool the city's society into thinking he was a Norwegian duke! And, he continued on as an impostor in order to land a wealthy young lady to wed – perhaps one that had just recently come into a large inheritance! And he would have gotten away with it, too, if it weren't for our scheme – which, in immediate retrospect, seemed less ingenious with every foot I was being dragged.

"And I stand here speaking for what I believe to be the interests of all citizens," Hughes began again.

As they threw me out of the main entrance, I landed on the floor next to a tall, gray-haired man who appeared to be having an argument with the staff member managing the admission table.

"I'm telling you, I am Benson Thatcher," the man insisted.

October 21, 1916

It will not surprise you at all, reader, to find out that Virginia no longer works at the Milwaukee Post newspaper.

The morning after the slight misunderstanding at the Hughes event, she tendered her immediate resignation. Within days, she had obtained a job setting up fundraisers for the Women's Temperance Movement, which vividly demonstrates how badly our plan backfired! Instead of dampening the moods of three men in her life, she has now been granted the authorization to make every man in America miserable!

I join Bertrand and Boomer for whiskey every now and then, and we commiserate about what exactly went wrong with the plan. (I maintain it all fell apart because Boomer's Norwegian accent was substandard.)

I still believe Virginia will one day be overcome by her secret love for me, but clearly, now is the time to let our relationship breathe. I could tell her my passion for her is similar to that of Frenchwoman Cecile Bourdier, who made her way to the front lines at the Somme in order to see her husband. Bourdier clipped her hair short, borrowed a French military uniform from a relative and snuck her way through the mud and bomb craters to the front lines. But, when trying to ask a sergeant where her "brother" was, a rat ran across her boot and she screamed, giving away the fact that she was a lady!

Bertrand has suggested a new FINGER-PHONE idea that he swears will make millions of dollars. Users would pay a monthly fee, then go on their device and order a book of their choosing. Then, someone would immediately call the customer and read the book to them.

Whoever heard of such a thing? Entertainment on demand! When people can just write their own books and have them read over the phone without needing printing and bookbinding, what will become of traditional book companies? What if publishers only sign contracts with authors who are FINGER-PHONE famous? I have recently seen one user brag that his cat can play the piano – this talented feline will probably get a book deal before a columnist with a popular newspaper will!

Fortunately, I have not heard anything from law enforcement in the weeks subsequent to my home being raided. This is odd, because I do actually harbor a strange fantasy of being falsely arrested for a murder I didn't commit.

For one, I believe I am excellent at arguing, and I am dying to demonstrate just how good I am by convincing everyone of my innocence while on the witness stand. Oh, how the newspapers would gush about the "charismatic man whose life has been torn asunder by spurious charges!"

Also, it would be nice to have it noted publicly that you actually have never killed anyone. What an aphrodisiac this would be for potential lady companions! How many men can prove definitively to a woman on their first date that he is not a murderer? I would wear a suit made of newspapers announcing my acquittal.

Despite all the terrible news in my life lately, there has been one exceedingly vivid ray of sunshine - Charles Evans Hughes is certain to win the presidency in two weeks!

In a special election in Maine last month, Republicans swept the state, winning everything on the ballot. And, as we all know, "As Maine goes, so goes the nation."

Both candidates have moved to the "hot campaigning" portion of the election season, where they hold no calumny back. This week, Woodrow Wilson accused Hughes of representing the "silent and secret" parts of the Republican Party and said that the GOP stands for "every form of bitterness" and "every ugly form of hate." Referring to former President Theodore Roosevelt, Wilson said the "only articulate voice" in the Republican Party "professes opinions and purposes at which the rest in private shiver and demur."

Wilson has also pushed the idea that the Republican Party will be split between Hughes loyalists and those secretly cheering for Roosevelt's more aggressive style of politics. But, any reader of the Milwaukee Post will know that the Republican Party is not as split as the LAMESTREAM MEDIA would have us all believe!

Even New York bookmakers have Justice Hughes as the prohibitive favorite; according to gamblers there, one must bet $5,000 to win $2,500 if Hughes wins - two to one odds against the incumbent!

This large lead is likely the result of Hughes' newfound acidity on the campaign trail. In his home state of New York last week, the Justice, "burning with indignation," savaged his critics, some of whom had criticized him for tossing aside his judgeship for the presidency.

"No American need apologize for being a candidate for office," said Hughes to loud cheers. "I had no desire to return to politics, but there came a summons which no honorable man could refuse."

Hughes has also had to answer accusations by Wilson that he has colluded with foreign interests in order to help his campaign. According to the president, Hughes has had secret meetings with both Germans and members of the Allied powers and made promises to each if he were to be elected.

"It is hardly necessary to say that if I am elected," Hughes told another New York crowd, "we shall have an exclusively American policy in the service of American interests."

"I have no secret understandings, no unstated purpose," Hughes told the crowd, adding that if anyone supposes that if he is elected "the right and interests of American citizens will be subordinated to any ulterior purpose or to the interest of the policies of any foreign power whatever, he is doomed to disappointment."

Even well before Election Day, Democrats are already charging voting fraud against Republicans. Yesterday, Assistant United States Attorney General Frank C. Dalley accused the GOP of busing over 300,000 black voters to Illinois, Indiana, and Ohio over the span of eighteen months in order to swing the elections in those states. As everyone knows, blacks vote overwhelmingly for Republicans, and Democrats hold a tight grip on the southern states. So it would make sense for the GOP to bring black voters north to ensure victory in states that are up for grabs.

Dalley, also a Wilson spokesman, called the Republican efforts a "gigantic voting fraud conspiracy" embracing the entire country. In Chicago alone, Democrats were able to strike 1,000 blacks from the city's voting rolls, claiming they had all registered to vote illegally.

Let us hope these black voters remain in the Midwest's big cities to continue voting overwhelmingly for Republicans for the next century!

Regardless of the Democrats' complaining, Hughes' election is all but ensured. On Friday, William R. Wilcox, chairman of the Republican national committee, declared that "the campaign is practically ended and there is nothing to it but the election of Hughes." Wilcox broke down the electoral votes for the media, showing that Hughes will win 308 votes, or forty-two in excess of the required 266 to become president. Further, he boasted that Republicans had over $1.6 million in the bank to run their campaigns around the country.

What a relief! According to the Post, Republicans outnumber the Democrats in America by more than one million voters. "It is only when the Republican Party is suffering from some untoward circumstance, such as operated against it four years ago, that the Democrats have any chance to win a national election," the paper said.

It is fortunate that residents of this city have a newspaper that will deliver them the truth about what is happening in politics! Unlike the city's Democratic papers, a Republican paper like the Post is more in tune with the thoughts of the regular people of America!

In just the past week, headlines in the paper have read "SWING FOR HUGHES SEEN IN ANALYSIS OF CONDITIONS IN

ALL STATES," "NATION SWINGS TO HUGHES," "HUGHES HOLDS INSIDE TRACK," "POLL SHOWS HUGHES LEADS IN ELECTORS," and "HUGHES IS ABSOLUTELY GOING TO WIN, AND EVEN IF HE DOESN'T IT'S NOT LIKE YOU'RE GOING TO BE ABLE TO EASILY LOOK UP THESE HEADLINES A CENTURY FROM NOW."

Most notably, the paper has emphasized how overwhelmingly Hughes has won over women and suffragists. In an article noting how much more politically active ladies are in 1916, the Post said women "now have reasons for thought, and they can express them wittily, sharply, briefly," and "to the point."

In a story I typed, the paper reported that over 4,000 women packed a Chicago auditorium on Thursday to see Theodore Roosevelt stump on Hughes' behalf. At the women's event, over a hundred ladies were brought to the stage to explain why they were for Hughes; many of them ridiculed Wilson's previous statements, claiming they backed Hughes because he wasn't "too proud to fight."

Further, the Post has gone out of its way to print photographs of all the pretty society women who support Justice Hughes' candidacy. The message is clear – vote for Hughes and some comely young lass will definitely want to pull the lever for YOU!

As it happens, in twelve backward states primarily in the West – Arizona, California, Colorado, Idaho, Illinois, Kansas, Montana, Nevada, Utah, Oregon, Washington, and Wyoming – women are ALLOWED to vote for president. Six of those states only allowed women's suffrage after 1912, so ladies in those states will be casting their first-ever presidential ballots.

That is why, in anticipation of Election Day, the national Republican Party has issued a list of instructions to help confused women vote on November 7th. The party told ladies it was safer to vote a "straight ticket," as that is far less perplexing than voting for different candidates from different parties.

"The slightest mistake in detail and the vote will be thrown out," reads the party's warning. "This is done every election with many man's votes, but to women, this first vote is too precious for them to want to take any chances."

Many people question the wisdom of a system whereby different newspapers espousing contrary political beliefs are allowed to exist. They complain that a city having a Republican newspaper and a Democratic newspaper makes each publication susceptible to printing FALSE NEWS.

But whoever heard of an "unbiased" newspaper? Since America's founding papers were created by businessmen with particular political leanings trying to influence voters, and ultimately, elections. A century ago, Federalist newspapers, promoting party leader John Adams, attacked Thomas Jefferson as an "Atheist," "anarchist," "demagogue," "coward," and "trickster," and said that Jefferson's followers were "cut-throats who walk in rags and sleep amid filth and vermin." And Jefferson was currently serving as Adams' vice-president!

Yet that was mundane politicking compared to the 1828 presidential race between Adams' son, John Quincy Adams, and Andrew Jackson. Jackson's supporters called Adams "The Pimp," based on a rumor about Adams coercing a young woman to have sex with a Russian Czar a decade earlier. Adams' supporters countered with a newspaper cartoon of Jackson hanging a man in a noose, a reference to Jackson's time spent executing Seminole Indian sympathizers. The cartoon's caption read, "Jackson is to be president and you will be HANGED."

The campaign also saw each candidate attack the other's wife. Jackson's supporters claimed that Louisa Adams was an illegitimate child that had been having intimate relations with Adams before marriage. Adams' supporters pointed out that Rachel Jackson married Andrew before her previous marriage had legally ended. After growing increasingly depressed, Rachel Jackson died several days after Jackson won the campaign, and Andrew never stopped blaming Adams for her death.

If partisan papers in the modern era craft news in a more favorable light for one candidate or the other, it certainly doesn't mean the end of democracy. Battles between partisan media empires have been far more vituperative in the past, and democracy is still very much alive!

While news of the presidential race has kept my mind off my failed attempts at romancing a lady, so has the slate of fascinating stories running across my desk at work. For instance, in Chicago, a young white girl was just taken from the home of a black woman who had raised the child since she was a week old.

Back in 1902, "Mammy" Camilla Jackson was working as a maid in Jacksonville, Florida when she was hired to care for a child by an actress named Mrs. Delbridge. The young actress was unable to nurse her newborn daughter, Marjorie, and "Mammy," who had spent a decade nursing white children, happily took the job.

When young Marjorie turned seven years old, Mrs. Delbridge tragically died, after having left her daughter in Mrs. Jackson's permanent care. When city authorities found out that Marjorie, now fourteen years old, was still in the care of a black woman, they ordered the white child removed. They immediately began searching for Marjorie's closest relative and, if they find none, they will place her with another white family.

What an injustice! It has broken poor Mammy's heart to have her child ripped from her grasp. In order to earn sympathy from the city, she even told court commissioners that she had never allowed Marjorie to associate with any colored folks other than her own children. What a humiliation she was willing to endure to simply get her baby back!

One even more troubling story crossed my desk yesterday - one that I simply couldn't believe was real. As reporter Dirk Callaway handed it to me in handwritten form, he shrugged and said, "I thought of all the people in the office, you might want to see this one."

He walked away and I read the article:

INVESTMENT BANKER ON THE LAM NABBED IN MISSOURI

Millionaire Michigan investment banker Bernard Wolfe was apprehended by law enforcement today in Joplin, Missouri, who immediately charged him with fraudulently manipulating stock prices. According to court documents, Wolfe had been unlawfully spreading misinformation to drive down the price of stocks, then purchasing those stocks at a reduced rate. Wolfe had been using his telephone line to mislead investors about the nature of the investments, making it a federal crime.

Wolfe has been traveling the country for the last several months, staying in hotels across America under the alias "Sebastian Schneider." Other hotel guests say "Schneider" had told them he was a sad, lonely newspaper employee who had once served as a spokesman for a drug that helped men with erectile dysfunction.

Wolfe told the court his arrest was simply a plot by the German government to weaken America's financial structure by taking down its most successful businessmen. When led to jail in handcuffs, he promised he would be pardoned by President Charles Evans Hughes, a man who would one day "Make America Great Again."

I gulped.

Clearly, Wolfe had used information from my INTER-LOG postings to steal my identity while he evaded capture! He was sharing details he could have only gleaned from reading my FINGER-PHONE communications. (Also, his characterization of me seemed a bit unnecessarily insulting.)

Had he known of my feelings for Grace all along? Did he know I knew of his secret dealings? Did he do any business in my name?

I had so many immediate questions. Most prominent among them – WHERE IS GRACE?

November 11, 1916

By now, you know what happened on Election Day. I will recount my story.

On Tuesday morning, I noticed news editor Oliver Pringle lurking by the staircase in the typists' room. This was an anomaly, as the kings in the newsroom typically treat the typists as if we were cholera-flavored cream of wheat.

"You there!" he barked through his cigar. "What's your name?"

"Schneider," I said. "Sebastian."

"Odd name. Well, Mr. Schneider Sebastian, how would you like to be a part of our election coverage tonight?"

Name transposition aside, I couldn't believe he chose me to join the vaunted newsroom for the evening! I had finally gotten my big break!

"I would love to, sir," I gleefully told him.

"Come with me," he said.

We went to his office and he sat me down.

"I'm skilled at talking to people, and I'm a fine writer," I told him, barely able to catch my breath.

"Settle down, son," he said, curling the ends of his thick, gray moustache. "You don't need a pen where you're going."

"Oh?"

"But almost 400,000 people will find out who the next president is because of you."

I was intrigued.

"On the roof of our building, we've set up a powerful searchlight and pointed it straight to the zenith. Our newsroom is set up with a dozen telegraph machines that will be sending us election results."

"Yes, sir."

"Don't interrupt me, son. While the result is still unknown, the searchlight beam will remain a neutral white. When the telegraphs tell us who won, you will change the color of the beam and alert the city's residents."

This seemed unlikely to launch my career as the next Upton Sinclair.

"If Hughes takes the lead, the beam will be green," he said. "If Wilson wins, you'll change it to red."

"Stop and go. Red and green. I understand," I said.

"Take the rest of the day off. It could be a late night for you," said Mr. Pringle. "Be back here at seven o'clock."

I went home and, rather than take a brief nap, I dialed up the FINGER-PHONE to tell everyone I knew that I would be the most famous man in the city for one evening! I simply told them to watch the sky to see my handiwork.

I returned to the office at seven and walked up the twenty flights of stairs to reach the roof. There were instructions on how to turn on the searchlight, along with colored glass to slide into place when the information changed.

I flipped the searchlight on, and it began humming loudly. I centered it skyward to the place I thought the most people could see it. And, as instructed, I waited for further word from the telegraph operators sixteen floors below me.

The wait was long and the night was cold. Sitting close to the light was the warmest spot on the roof. I took solace in the fact that I would be providing so many people with information; this was much better than working in a much smaller city like Los Angeles. I would often walk to the ledge and look down at the tiny people below, who all had their necks craned upward to see the beam of light. Some even waved to me.

Maybe there's a girl out there that will one day be impressed that I was "the light guy!"

As I waited, I read the day's paper – knowing none of the stories contained within would approach the impact of the one I was working on.

Yesterday, a local girl had to go to court to defend herself against a charge of being "too pretty." Last Wednesday, Miss Katherine Borre, daughter of a local politician, was walking home from the store with her arms full of milk and a music roll, when local twenty-one-year-old automobile salesman Raymond Burgert asked if she needed help carrying her items.

She said no, at which point Burgert took advantage of her arms being full and caught Borre in an unexpected lip blizzard. When Borre complained to police, Burgert responded that he was the victim, as Borre had "assaulted his eyes with her beauty."

In court, Borre took the stand and told the judge that she didn't think she was really pretty enough for a man to do that to her. "Nonsense!" yelled the judge, who, for the sake of her own self-esteem, insisted she watch the rest of the trial sitting on his lap.

As I looked up from my newspaper, I gasped. It appears other newspapers had gotten the same idea and put up their own searchlights to announce the election result! Another beam of light emanated from a nearby downtown building, presumably from the Milwaukee Journal. (I assumed it didn't come from the Butter, Egg, and Cheese Journal, as they would only alert voters if a Holstein had been picked to run the Department of Justice.)

It was nearly ten in the evening, and I ran to the door to the stairs to alert the editors that their idea had been boosted. Just then, a secretary sprung from the door and handed me a piece of paper.

I turned from her, knowing it was the most important piece of paper I'd ever hold in my life.

I unfolded it, and it simply said one word: Hughes.

I immediately turned the searchlight off and slid the green filter into place. Just as I turned the light back on, I noticed the other beam change, as well.

Only this beam was red!

Perhaps the Journal was playing dirty and trying to ruin our scheme;

maybe, being a paper for Democrats, they considered Hughes the "stop" and Wilson the "go," and they were actually reporting the same findings we were. Either way, people sitting on their roofs at home wouldn't stand a chance of interpreting which beam of light was which.

I ran down and told Mr. Pringle that our competitors were engaging in subterfuge. He told me to leave the light and go home; the first edition of the paper would be out in mere hours and then people would know for certain that Justice Charles Evans Hughes was their new president.

Sure enough, as I woke on Wednesday morning, there was the banner headline in the Post: "HUGHES LEADS IN HOT FIGHT." Underneath the headline was a large picture of the bald, bearded Hughes – the same one whose speech I had interrupted just last month – with the caption, "The Probable President-Elect." Further down the page was a photo of the Hughes family labeled "It Looks As If They Would Occupy the White House."

However, as you know, reader, the only way Charles Evans Hughes will enter the White House is if he pays to take the tour.

Oh, how I wish I had not bragged about being the "light guy!" On Wednesday, I was savaged on the FINGER-PHONE for allegedly having shone the wrong light color, indicating a Wilson win – even though it was the Milwaukee Journal that did so! On Thursday, as it became clear Wilson was, in fact, the winner, I was then harangued for getting the original Hughes call wrong! I was FALSE NEWS!

On Thursday morning, as results from the western states began to trickle in, it was clear President Woodrow was pulling ahead. As early as Friday, a local men's clothing store taunted Hughes supporters by running a newspaper ad blaring, "I TOLD YOU SO!" and that "A Square Deal Always Wins Out!" (Also, men's suits are evidently available for fifteen dollars.)

On Friday morning, I had to push my way through a throng of protesters in order to get to the paper's front door. Over 2,500 people had shown up at the Milwaukee Post to taunt the paper for its pro-Hughes coverage. Carrying signs and shouting through bullhorns, demonstrators screamed "Wilson!" loud enough for reporters and editors to hear them.

The paper, of course, had fun with the protesters, running an article claiming they only deigned the Post worthy of demonstration because it is the "World's Greatest Newspaper." The article described the jibes being sent the paper's way as "good-natured" and "effervescent."

Others were not as ready to play nice in the wake of Hughes' defeat. My paper blamed Hughes himself for not traveling to California and meeting with progressive Governor Hiram Johnson, who could have helped the Justice lock down votes in the state. Moreover, the paper shredded the citizens of California themselves for favoring Wilson and denying Hughes the presidency.

"By giving Wilson the vote it did, California, with its record and Wilson's record, presented itself as the champion boob state of the American republic," a Friday editorial read.

Yet, we must save our enmity for the true culprit! Wilson won ten of the twelve states in which women could vote – it was likely the ladies that carried old Woodrow to victory!

Thus, the score was WOMEN 1, SEBASTIAN 0 – an outcome

that seemed destined for my gravestone!

In fact, with my scheme to use my lighting prowess to attract the fairer sex having backfired, I decided it may be time to find female companionship on the FINGER-PHONE.

In the past year, an untold amount INTER-LOGS have been created to match prospective lovers with someone of their own, very specific taste. Unable to find one where I could order up a female that matched my parameters (a redheaded marching band drummer), I finally settled on SANGUINE PEOPLE MEET DOT NET DOT BIZ.

At first, the questions meant to match me with a lady seemed intrusive, but I answered them to the best of my knowledge.

"How many of your limbs do you still have?"

All of them?

"What is your pet peeve?"

People who use the term "stool culture," as it is an oxymoron.

"How many days a week do you feel overcome by the grip?"

No more than two.

"How many of your teeth do you still have?"

Most of them, I think?

"What is your favorite book?"

The dictionary! I am still hoping they make a movie adaptation with Charlie Chaplin playing the role of a semicolon.

"How many of your siblings have succumbed to tuberculosis? A) 2, B) 3, or C) 4 or more"

N/A

"Are you a robot? Please type in these letters for us to confirm you are not: Q8LGH3MS."

Q8LGH3MS

(Although, if there are any lady robots out there, I would hope they'd be impressed by my efficiency and accuracy in typing those letters in.)

I was thankful the questions didn't get too autobiographical, as what women don't know about men is our best feature. But I felt humor was definitely important, as jokes are for boys like boobs are for girls. If you have good ones, you get far more attention than you deserve.

In any event, it took days for my FINGER-PHONE to spit out a match. Who knows? Perhaps my beloved WillieCat was out there searching for me and was secretly using a dating account as an anonymous way to set up a clandestine meeting!

The woman to whom I was matched was allegedly named "Ruth" - which could have easily been a code from Grace. During one discussion with her in June, I set off on a long diatribe about the word "ruthless," wondering aloud what exactly "ruth" was, and why you were a cretin if you didn't have any of it. We laughed together as I explained how I was going to find this "ruth," mine it as if it was a precious metal, and sell it to wretched people to make them sufferable in public!

This "Ruth" was supposedly twenty-one years old, making her a

"Centennial" – one of the new breed of spoiled young adults ruining society. Clearly, the generation of men and women who came of age around 1900 have it too easy. They wait until the old age of twenty-two to get married, they refuse to walk more than four hours to get to work, and their lax morals often lead them to slow dance with one another before the twelfth date!

The website informed me I was to meet Ruth for lunch at Antonin's Italian restaurant on Eighth Street on Thursday morning. I thought I could get away from work long enough to make this date happen, especially if it were truly my beloved Grace.

At noon, I snuck away from my Linotype and made my way to Antonin's. I picked up flowers on the way, knowing Grace would be impressed by the gesture – even if it literally is the show of love that requires the least thought or effort.

I bounded into the restaurant, where I saw a young woman sitting by herself reading pages that appeared to have come from a FINGER-PHONE. She was reasonably attractive, with long black hair and a bit of a receding chin. I walked over and stood next to her table while she read. She did not look up.

I coughed.

"Yes?" she said.

"I'm Sebastian," I answered, taking her hand.

"Oh, hello. I'm Ruth. Please sit," she said, without standing herself.

I pulled my chair out and settled in, expecting to make conversation. Yet she continued to read the pages in front of her as if I was not even there. As we sat in silence, I noticed an odd sight on top of the bar. It appeared as if she brought her FINGER-PHONE to the restaurant and plugged it into the restaurant's phone line in order to receive messages as we ate!

Minutes passed as I stewed over this woman not being my WillieCat. At no point during this silence did she recognize me or beg my pardon for her preoccupation. Is this expected on dates now?

"My device tells me we have a great deal in common," I said. "We are both not Eskimos, neither of us wears an eyepatch, and neither of us has ever been involved in any international conspiracies involving the smuggling of Tungsten." She was getting my A-plus material.

"Huh? What's that again?" she said, looking up briefly.

"Tungsten," I said.

"Oh."

"Chemical symbol of 'W' for some reason."

"Oh. You know you're sort of old?"

"Uh, yes."

Another minute of silence.

"I have the weirdest job – I'm a 'clother' at a red-light district establishment," I said. "I run on stage naked, and women throw money at me to put my clothes back on."

"Oh."

"You're not listening to me, are you?"

"Oh."

"That reminds me. Does the word 'embarrassed' come from the compound of 'bare-assed?' Because I can't think of many times being bare-assed wouldn't be embarrassing."

"I have to go to the ladies' room," she said as she got up, walked toward the lavatory, and stopped to remove more fresh papers from her portable FINGER-PHONE.

I couldn't possibly be expected to refrain from peeking at the papers she had been reading. As I slid several sheets toward my side of the table, I noticed she had been reading other people's dating profiles!

While on a date with me, she was contemplating other man-options!

I immediately pushed the papers back to her placemat and settled in to give her a piece of the old Schneider mind when she returned. We had not yet even ordered food, but I was set to give her some verbal vinegar!

She returned and sat in her chair.

"You want to just get out of here and go to my place?" she said.

I immediately applied the brakes to my emotional jeremiad.

"To your house?" I said.

"Yes, dummy," she answered.

How my mind raced! Her offer was entirely inappropriate –

being alone in a residence with a lady is a fourth date transgression at best. But how I longed for the companionship of a woman! But what would become of me if I were to betray my conscience? How would I be able to live with myself if I were to consummate a relationship with a lady with whom I had barely exchanged a word?

This period of contemplation lasted approximately three-tenths of a second.

"Absolutely. Let's go," I said.

Like any gentleman would, I carried her FINGER-PHONE back to her apartment, which was only two blocks away. I nearly slipped on the ice several times.

As we entered the apartment, she told me to have a seat on the couch while she "got ready." She disappeared into her bedroom as I once again battled guilt. But given my trouble attracting the ladies, when was a chance like this going to come around again? In recent years, I could have been hiding the cure for childhood typhoid in my pants, and I wouldn't have been able to get a girl to investigate it. Who was I kidding? I would push a wheelbarrow of anvils across Arkansas to make this happen.

She emerged from her room wearing a white silken gown trimmed with lace. The bottom rose just above her alabaster calves, exposing her bare feet and ankles.

She walked toward me and put her hands on my shoulders. I thought of Grace and whether she would approve of my being right here, right now. But who knows where she was? She could be in prison, or dead, or searching for Pancho Villa in Mexico!

Ruth wrapped her arms around my neck and pulled my chest together with hers. If my heart had been hooked up to the city's electrical grid, it could have powered Milwaukee for a month.

"The joke about Tungsten was awful," she whispered to me, moving her face closer.

"I find chemicals with odd symbols fascinating," I whispered delicately in her ear. "Like, how did Sodium end up with 'Na'?"

"Please stop talking now," she said, pulling even nearer.

Her sweet breath tickled my moustache. The possibility that this was an elaborate prank being played on me by Philly seemed increasingly minute.

Just then, there was a calamitous banging on her front door.

"POLICE!" someone yelled. "Open up!"

The banging continued.

"One second!" yelled Ruth, running into her room to slip into her housecoat.

How did the police know I was here? Could they have picked a worse time? Was I about to be pummeled into the floor of this apartment? (It appeared I was concealing a billy club of my own in my drawers - they might take it as a threat!)

Ruth opened the door, and two officers walked in.

"Ma'am, there's a crackdown on truancy going on in this neighborhood, and we saw you enter the building with that young man right there." There was a tall officer with a large, square head and a red complexion that made him look like a fireplace. He pointed at me.

"Truancy?" I said, puzzled.

"Yes – a lot of high school students have been ditching school, and we have been tasked to find them. Just what are you two doing here in the middle of the day?" he asked.

"I was here to fix her typewriter," I said, pointing at the FINGER-PHONE.

"He must really like fixing typewriters," joked the shorter cop, perhaps noticing I was holding a copy of the Milwaukee Post over my lower abdomen. They both laughed.

I scanned the room. Ruth was gone.

"What's your name, son?"

"I'm twenty-seven years old," I said.

"That's not what we asked."

As a fugitive from the law, I thought it best to not divulge my identity. My mind raced.

"Albert," I said. "Sharpton."

"Can we see some identification, Mr. Al Sharpton?" the fireplace asked.

I took a step back and once again sat on the couch. Like Sherlock Holmes, I tried to sense every angle of the room at once to see how I might get out of this without divulging my identity. The window was closed, and we were on the third floor, so I could not simply dive out. The officers were blocking the door, so making a run for it that way would lead to facial bruising at best. I began sweating like a pig at a bacon raffle. As Holmes would say, it was quite the "three pipe problem."

Just then, a third officer burst into the room. "I think I found a suspect," he said, breathing heavily.

"What does he look like?" asked the fireplace.

"Woman, gray hair, walking with a cane, had a cat on a leash."

"The perfect disguise!" yelled shorty cop.

"It's your lucky day, Sharpton," said brickhead. "Get back to class."

"I'm twenty-s– oh, never mind. Yes sir," I said.

"Good boy."

All the officers filed out to take down an elderly woman they believed was skipping out on sophomore English class.

I rose from the couch, looked around, and poked my head into Ruth's bedroom. She glanced up from her FINGER-PHONE, which she had been checking as I very narrowly escaped the electric chair.

"Why are you still here?" she asked, stone-faced.

"Oh," I said. "Um."

"My brother will be home any minute – you have to go," she said.

I put my overcoat on, slouched, and dragged myself out the front door. I took solace in the fact I would one day have a risible story to tell at parties. Just wait until they hear about the time I was "cop blocked!" What an unforgivable abuse of the penal system!

December 9, 1916

In the past month, I have come to learn the word "anhedonia." It is a condition in which a person is unable to find pleasure in any activity, no matter how exciting. Every day, I feel as if I have woken up on the wrong side of the bed – the inside.

It has been a punishing string of disappointments that has made me unable to function in the world outside my home. The prospect of Woodrow Wilson being president for four more years is as enticing as wearing a hat made of hard-boiled eggs. In addition to Wilson's victory, "dry" candidates favoring the prohibition of alcohol won all over America. In twenty-five of the forty-eight states, voters have either passed referendums in favor of going dry or have elected legislatures that have banned alcohol altogether.

If this type of momentum remains, America will soon be a place where an honest man cannot even go enjoy a beer after work! Banning liquor of all kinds won't make your life longer – it will only seem longer!

Only adding to my malaise is the demonic FINGER-PHONE, which has reduced my attention span to that of a mouse who has fallen into a sugar pot. As information spews forth like a fire hose, it is now impossible to tell which news is important and what is mere fantasy.

Further, I have found myself irritable when I consider my standing among other FINGER-PHONE users. It is a demonstrable fact that, whenever a new society is formed, human beings begin to rank one another and fight for their place in the upper strata. INTER-LOGS are no different. For instance, when less deserving users have more "followers" than I do, I want to begin chewing my belt leather in anger!

As with any other social group, certain members must assert their dominance in the upper reaches of the "statusphere." On the FINGER-PHONE, that dominance is quantified in influence and followers. The new currency isn't dollars – it is attention!

But, the primary cause of my eternal sadness is my lack of a female companion. It is true, the INTER-LOGS introduced me to WillieCat in the first place; without it, I would have never felt the joy of being important to someone whom I adored so completely. But it also demonstrated that specific type of love is ephemeral. With the snip of a phone cord, your heart can turn grey. (And yours truly aside, how many men miss out on what is right in front of their eyes while pursuing such fleeting, fantastical love on their FINGER-PHONES?)

Oddly, the best advice for wooing women in person may be coming from one of America's worst people. Last week, Charles H. Wax of New York was arrested for swindling over three hundred women out of money and property. Wax, typically using a pseudonym, would bait women into a relationship, then bleed them dry of their riches.

Once in custody, Wax revealed all the secrets that allowed him, a former plumber, to earn the love of hundreds of ladies. It turns out he had written formulas specially crafted to different sorts of women. If a specific formula failed to attract a specific lady, he would simply try others until one would.

First in Wax's bag of tricks – he would immediately propose to a woman, typically at their first meeting. Sometimes, he would ask a female's hand in marriage within five minutes of meeting them.

"I tell 'em I love 'em as soon as I meet 'em," said Wax from prison. "They all fall for it. The pretty girl accepts it as she does a seat in the streetcar – as coming to her. To the homely one, it is the flattery her soul craves. She believes the poor gink has fallen a victim to her fatal fascinations."

"I have made love to waitresses and women who wore diamonds and drove their own cars. They're all alike."

Wax also believed it was important to dress well. "With women, the clothes make the man," he said. "An eleven-dollar suit of clothes, a pair of nose glasses, yellow gloves, gray spats, a walking stick, and a chrysanthemum in the buttonhole will make a waiter or a barber look like a millionaire."

What if someone were to use these secrets for the powers of good and not evil? I only need one lady – that is two hundred and ninety-nine fewer than Charlie Wax was able to tempt!

I scrawled a few words on a crumpled piece of paper, forming a rudimentary shopping list. "Nose glasses. Chrysanthemum. Spats." I wasn't sure where one could purchase these upscale personal adornments, so I looked it up on the FINGER-PHONE. It turns out there was a Walking Stick, Spat, and Beyond store just six blocks from my house.

I put on my overcoat, walked outside, and began shuffling to the store. I wasn't more than three blocks from my front door when I saw a familiar face crossing the same intersection.

It was Virginia.

I nodded at her, hoping a simple act of recognition would suffice. But she walked toward me, stopping within three feet of my nose.

"Hello," I said.

"How are you doing?" she said.

"I guess I've been better," I said, focusing my eyes downward and kicking a dirty patch of snow on the ground. "I heard you have a new job. I'd wish you luck, but I kind of hope you don't succeed."

"Ha, yes – I am aware of your feelings on banning alcohol," she said. "I think all of Milwaukee is aware of your position at this point, Shaq Diesel."

I cracked a faint smile.

"I really apologize for what happened at the Hughes event," I said. "If you think about it, it probably helped you – kept you from wasting your time."

"I know," she said. "I am aware that was all Bertrand's plan. You can be a pretty good guy when you want to be," she said. "There were times I could actually see myself with you more so than the other two," she said.

My heart leapt.

"Although, I think maybe in the future, we should be buddies," she said. "I'm actually dating someone right now and I really like him."

It took me a moment to recover from this uppercut.

"What does he do?" I said.

"He's a businessman," she answered. "Started a store selling coats - but only the sleeves from the coats. He's well on his way to being a millionaire," she said.

I gulped.

"I'm very happy for you," I said. I was not very happy for her.

"Well, I hope we get to run into one another again soon," she said with a melancholy half-smile.

"If you look up Milwaukee on a map, that's where I'll be," I said. "Don't look at Texas or North Dakota, because I won't be in those places. Or California, New Hampshire, Maine, Arizona, Oklahoma, Arkansas, Alabama, Nebraska, Guam, New Guinea, Ohio, Pakistan, or the small African Nation of Chad. I won't be at any of those places. Just in Milwaukee."

"Seriously, are you feeling okay?" she asked.

"I've been better," I replied.

"Well, I do hope you take care of yourself," she said, bundling herself tighter.

"Okay."

"Wait, one more thing," she said. "What was that magic box

thing Bertrand was talking about?"

"You know how you send letters?" I answered. "It's like that. You can just send them right away and to anyone around the country."

"Oh! Maybe I'll get one!" she said. "Then I'll send you a phone letter!"

"I wouldn't recommend–"

"Just think of how much smarter and happier everyone will be!" she chirped.

"Yes. I suppose you're right," I said.

She waved, turned, and disappeared into the snow, which was now being illuminated by the street lights.

Sans spats, I walked home and crawled into bed. I tried to think of possible solutions to my loneliness. I needed a boost to my self-esteem, but I reminded myself of my longstanding theory that many people with low self-esteem also happen to be right.

I considered logging on to the FINGER-PHONE to take my mind off of things, but that would simply be swapping one form of misery for another.

I picked up the newspaper and read the story about divorced women who are forming their own "divorce colonies" around America to support one another after they split from their husbands. Perhaps the same thing could work for loveless twenty-seven-year-old men. Instead of sitting home and waiting for the sweet release of death, we could do masculine things together – like spending time talking about searing juices into meats.

As night fell, I melted into my bed, feeling my senses drift into sleep. But then, I heard a heavy banging on my door. I wasn't expecting anybody.

"Who is it?" I yelled.

The banging commenced again.

I pulled myself out of bed, as expletives fell from my mouth like oats from a horse.

"Who is it" I asked again.

No answer.

"WHAT DO YOU WANT?"

I heard a faint, feminine voice from the other side of the door.

"I want to hold your beer while you do something temporarily inadvisable."

My body went numb. I swung the door open.

It was Grace.

She ran in and leapt into my arms, squeezing me tightly.

"I never thought you'd come!" I said.

"I never thought I'd be able to," she answered, nearly out of breath.

For living a feral life on the lam, she was more beautiful than I even remembered her. If used in the European war, she could have been the Allies' most potent weapon against the Central Powers - send her to any battlefield and the enemy would melt in their shoes.

"How I've missed you!" I yelled, barely able to control the volume of my voice.

"And I, you," she said. "But we have plenty of time to talk about this later. We have to get moving."

"Did the police follow you here?" I said.

"I don't think so, but listen carefully. While he evaded the police, my husband tried to hide his millions of dollars from detection," she said. "He left great sums in bank accounts all over the country, from Indiana to Kentucky to Mississippi."

"And who has that money now?" I said.

"That's the kicker. He left all the money under the pseudonym 'Sebastian Schneider.'"

"Yes, I read that."

"Are you not understanding this?" she asked. "You can collect that money!"

"You want to live together as wealthy people?" I said, dumbfounded, wondering whether Grace's sudden appearance at my home was solely for financial reasons.

"I would like nothing more," she said. "But we need to get moving now."

I walked toward her and put the back of my hand on her soft face. I had dreamed about this moment for as long as I knew she was a woman.

I pulled her closer. I started to close my eyes. We both tilted our heads to our respective right.

Just before my eyes closed, I saw a red flashing light on the brick building outside my window. I released Grace from my grasp and ran to see what was going on.

It was the police. The building appears to be surrounded.

I have run to my FINGER-PHONE to quickly finish off this post with the events of the past five minutes for posterity. Right now, Grace is standing over me with her hand on my shoulder.

There is no escape.

There is a knock on the door.

I should go answer it.

About the Author

Christian Schneider has spent time as a political columnist at *USA Today*, the *Milwaukee Journal Sentinel*, and *National Review Online*. His op-eds have been featured in *The New York Times*, *Wall Street Journal*, *New York Post*, *City Journal* magazine, *Weekly Standard* magazine, and *National Review* magazine. He has been a frequent guest on political television and radio shows, having appeared on CNN, MSNBC, and Headline News. He holds a Master's degree in political science from Marquette University and lives in Madison, Wisconsin.

Acknowlegments

It is a universal truth that telling people you're writing a book is far superior to actually writing a book. The former takes mere seconds, as you explain your brilliant book premise and soak in the adoration of the listener. The latter takes months of pounding diet soft drinks at two in the morning, huddled over a keyboard in your basement, stringing together sentences you're never sure anyone will read. As Stephen Fry once put it, "Writing, ghastly at the time but great afterwards, is exactly the opposite of sex."

More importantly, you can only use the "I'm writing a book" trick once per person – once a friend hears those words from you, the next time you bring it up should be the point at which you are handing them their own copy. Otherwise, they will know you have bamboozled them into temporary adoration, at which point you will need to point out your dog is a rescue dog in order to restore your ethical standing.

As I learned these lessons, there are plenty of people who put up with me yammering on about my unfinished book. Most importantly, thanks to my parents, who miraculously were able to meet and birth me without a dating app. Thanks to Morgan and the kids, who are probably still wondering what daddy was doing in the basement all those hours.

Thanks to the Wisconsin Historical Society for making so many old newspapers easy to search. Thanks to Patrick Marley, Jason Stein, and Ernie Franzen for reading early drafts and suggesting the book needed an actual story. Thank you to Karyn Riddle for reading a late draft and confirming that I hadn't wasted all my time.

Thanks to Davy Rothbart for his generosity in showing me how to run the book game. Thanks to Barrett Kilmer and Heather Wilhelm for keeping their eye-rolls to a minimum as I discussed my manuscript. (And began using words like "manuscript.")

Thank you to P.G. Wodehouse for being the best English language novelist of the 20th century.

Finally, special thanks to Taryn Wieland for her proofreading and editing skills.

I read one "how to write a book" website that counseled in favor of adding a "suggested discussion topics" list at the end of your novel, to give potential book clubs some themes to debate. Seeing as how this book has no themes and offers no life lessons, be warned: If your book group says they want to discuss it, it is a trap. They are tricking you into attending an intervention. (Hopefully for an addiction to buying too many books.)

51312086R00156

Made in the USA
Middletown, DE
01 July 2019